The Vajrapani Institute Cookbook

Recipes and Reflections

from a Tibetan Buddhist Retreat Center

Book design & Illustrations by Alexandra Stein
Compiled by Nina Tomkiewicz
Edited by Wanda Sisnroy
Photographs courtesy of Vajrapani Institute, Elaine Jackson, Shasta Wallace, and Chris Wessleman

DEDICATION

∞

This book is dedicated to all living beings:
To their inward search,
To the liberation from their struggles,
And to the success of their happiness.

To all those beings who give their energy
So that life may be sustained.
For all those who grow, harvest, transport, and prepare the food we eat every day,
May they each receive boundless blessings.
And through our activities of cooking and eating this delicious food,
May these blessings last until all of us actualize our highest potential.

Enlightenment is not just chocolate at the end, in a lump.
It is chocolate, chocolate, chocolate all the way!

~ Lama Yeshe

TABLE OF CONTENTS

Cooking with the Heart:
The Story of the Vajrapani Institute Kitchen

Vajrapani Institute's (VPI) inception as a retreat center goes back to 1977, when devotees of Lama Yeshe lived in teepees on the land; an open field covered by a parachute served as their makeshift gompa. The property was generously donated by neighbors at OMland, and in the beginning days, there were no buildings – just very inspired and devoted individuals, pursuing the dharma and serving their Lama.

At that time, food was cooked for those living on the land at both the "Jackson Kitchen" and "Ridge Kitchen" (pictured on the next page). Food was prepared on wood-fired stoves to serve those who offered service by developing the land. Neither kitchen functions as a kitchen any longer: the Jackson Kitchen has since been built upon and now is a fully lived-in cabin, while the Ridge Kitchen has become a private retreat destination on Lama's Ridge – Cabin #2.

In 1981, construction began on what is today's kitchen at VPI. It began to be used in 1982, though at the time it did not yet have a roof or all of its counters in place. In 1983, the gompa above the kitchen was completed, which meant the kitchen now had a roof. Centrally located on the land, and equipped with propane stoves and ovens and fridges, the kitchen is able to serve all kinds of practitioners who come through to work, serve, learn, meditate, and grow.

In the early days, everything was made from scratch: the yogurt, bread, granola, crackers, and even tofu, as these items weren't as readily available to us as they are today. We still make our own Vajrapani granola though (and you'll find the recipe for it in this book!), and on the days it bakes inside the oven, you'll discover a faint smell of cinnamon wafting around the land.

9

Always vegetarian in nature, the VPI kitchen has kept meals simple, nourishing, and grounding to be of most support for the meditators coming through. Food that is too heavy, rich, or fancy could distract us from spiritual practice and disrupt our meditation. That being said, the meals are wholesome and satisfying, and those who take the time to prepare the food have loving hands and big hearts. VPI's environment supports internal exploration, or an uncovering and rediscovering of our inherent nature: that of a boundless goodness. In essence, kitchens are heart-spaces, and from the kitchen we provide loving support to nourish these transformational processes. Going on a meditation retreat is an endeavor like jumping into the unknown, and having nourishing food with familiar tastes and smells is a way to ground us in this process.

Whether the kitchen was a cookstove, a roofless construction site, or a finished building, the quality of the cook's hearts at VPI hasn't changed a bit. And perhaps this is the most important ingredient when cooking for others: maintaining calmness, and infusing the food with that peace of mind.

Vajrapani Institute's Cooks Throughout the Years

The kitchen at VPI would not be able to accomplish much without the dedication and hard work of its cooks. Those who prepare and serve food at VPI are motivated by the desire to support our patron's journeys on the spiritual path. All those who serve at VPI are integral in creating such an environment for spiritual development, and so it is in part because of the cook's nourishing support that our visitors are able to take the time to go inward. The following list of cooks at VPI over the years is a way to recognize the myriad of precious beings who have given in this way:

- Shasta Wallace
- Jean Smithfield
- Rose Kamin
- Pelgye, aka John Douthitt
- Mary Advey
- Roger Munroe
- Hope White
- Jim Davidson
- Shannon McGinnis
- Ben Walsch
- Gayle Kennedy
- Maureen Nelly
- Catherine Whiteley
- Janice Allen
- Llary Zang
- Venerable Angie
- Age Del Banco
- Ariel Howe
- Angelica Walker
- Fenix Bedoya
- Cynthia Koontz
- Heidi Oehler
- Kendra Hanson
- Ben Kalayjian
- Judy Davis
- Kimo Elliott
- James Kirk
- Amanda Karg
- Lori Holetz
- Karl Noonan
- Kelli Peacock
- Ruth Saro
- Nina Tomkiewicz

INTRODUCTION

Recipes serve as reminders until we don't need them anymore. After cooking for a number of years, I find it hard to believe that I've ever not known how to cook a pot of rice. Or that I used to have my nose in a cookbook in order to make a batch of cookies. That, of course, is me taking for granted all the remembering I have had to do, again and again, day after day, in order for these recipes to become a part of my daily habit. I firmly believe we all already know how to cook; recipes are our reminders of how to nourish ourselves, and we use them until we don't need them anymore. We read, we study, we practice – and then, we take this knowledge with us wherever we go. We build on it, we expand upon it, and we never cease practicing or learning. In this way cooking is very much its own form spiritual practice, isn't it?

Nevertheless, we can always re-visit what we thought we knew, or understand a different way of doing. Once we "know" how to make a pot of rice, the practice itself is always a fresh beginning and a new opportunity to make the rice delicious and fluffy. Each time, the grains of rice are grains we have never touched before, the pot is one day older, and the water is new to us, too. In this way, recipes can never remind us enough of what we already know.

Though Lama Yeshe passed away in 1984, his warmth towards others and desire to create an inclusive and comfortable environment is still very much alive at Vajrapani Institute. In the kitchen, we aim to cook in this spirit. Cooking with spirit means that your whole being is focused on your practice. Food can be an intensely social experience as well, bringing many people into the whole process. And while it may sound ephemeral and ungraspable conceptually, often we say that we have added the ingredient of "love" into the food, which personally is a way of translating my motivation when I cook: to take care of you.

I find that recipes serve best as guidelines to cooking, rather than restrictive boundaries squandering one's personal creativity. The simplicity of the ingredients and the steps involved in the following recipes allow you to dive in and feel your way around, comfortably. The truth is, recipes can always be expanded and enlivened further, yet the inspiration to nourish must begin within you, and it should not be scared away by elaborate ingredient lists and confusing instructions.

Many of the recipes in this book are gluten-free and vegan. There's an article in the back of the book that will expand on substitutions so that you can create your own gluten-free and vegan meals out of conventional recipes. Though eating this type of diet is not a necessity for optimum health, we've found that many of our patrons choose these diets to best support their bodies.

It's also worth noting that cooking involves more than just throwing ingredients together. There's a spirit behind it as well, a creative and loving spirit that will translate clearly through the food. Though it's true this cookbook is filled with recipes, we are hoping you delight in the joy of cooking itself, and may these recipes be a way for you to celebrate.

In addition to the recipes in this book you will also find articles and stories from people who have lived, taught, and/or worked at VPI. Stories about cooking for yourself while on retreat, and how to bring spirituality into your kitchen practices, both with preparation and consumption. You will read about the view from vegetarianism, and explore what it means to "get enough protein" with a vegetarian lifestyle.

The book is broken into various sections (such as Grains, Vegetables, Vegetarian Protein, etc.) which can collectively become the make-up of any meal in totality. Each part serves a function as far as nutritive value and physical support, and our bodies appreciate what each category has to offer. That being said, cooking need not be compartmentalized in this way, but I have personally found it easier to understand the various components of a nutritious meal by delineating food types in this way.

This book began as an idea ignited back in April 2014, and has only been able to blossom through the efforts of so many hands, so many hearts, and so much passion behind what the kitchen here does. Everyone I've met at VPI has served to invoke my own desire to nourish others in body and soul. Documenting recipes and bringing together this cookbook has been my labor of love for VPI, and my hope is that it is built upon as the center grows and evolves. May this book inspire your creativity and confidence in nourishing others, one of the most beautiful gifts to practice giving.

Nina Tomkiewicz
VPI Kitchen Manager & Cook
BOULDER CREEK, CA
APRIL 2015

∞

"Buddhas come from bodhisattvas, bodhisattvas come from bodhicitta and bodhicitta comes from great compassion. Great compassion comes from every single obscured suffering sentient being."

∞

How to Use Cooking in the Path
by Lama Zopa Rinpoche

The initial reason why people come to a Dharma center is not for the food but for the teachings and meditations; they are a little bored with the lives they have and are looking for something new. However, the conditions at the center, and especially the food, are a very important support for the teachings and meditations. Sometimes in the past, for example, when I would teach on impermanence, the hells, and the eight worldly dharmas, people would get scared and leave; but if the food was good they would stay. That's one way to keep them!

So I've been thinking for many days to come to the kitchen and explain a short meditation to the cooks. There is a short morning motivation I have put together with a direct meditation on the graduated path to the peerless happiness of full enlightenment followed by some verses explaining how precious and kind sentient beings are. Most of the time in English we use the expression "fully enlightened" but in Tibetan it is "sang gye;" 'sang' means that all the obscurations, gross and subtle have been purified, and 'gye' that all the realizations have been fully developed and there is nothing more to achieve. "Fully enlightened" has a different meaning; it's better to say "fully omniscient mind."

Every single sentient being is most precious, dear and wish-fulfilling; fulfilling all your wishes for the happiness of future lives, liberation, and enlightenment. Every hell being, hungry ghost, animal, insect, ant, mosquito, bird, goat, human being, sura and asura does this. That is because all our beginningless past lives' happiness, present happiness and future happiness comes from good karma and that good karma comes from your mind, from mental intention. Buddha's enlightened activity is of two types; one comes from Buddha's holy mind and one from your mind. Buddhas come from bodhisattvas, bodhisattvas come from bodhicitta and bodhicitta comes from great compassion. Great compassion comes from every single obscured suffering sentient being. There is no way to generate great compassion without depending on every single suffering sentient being. Therefore there is no bodhicitta, no bodhisattva, no Buddha and no way to create good karma, the cause of happiness, without them. In other words, every single happiness and comfort comes from sentient beings, even a cool breeze or a drink of water when you are thirsty. Without sentient beings there is no way to experience happiness in this life, future lives, liberation, or enlightenment. All our happiness comes from every single sentient being.

For example, all my happiness comes from every one of you and from all the rest of the sentient beings; every hell being, hungry ghost, animal, human, sura and asura. All my past, present and future happiness comes from everyone because Buddha, Dharma and Sangha in whom I take refuge and with whom I purify every single negative karma and achieve the peerless happiness of full enlightenment come from everyone. That is why sentient beings are most kind, dear, precious and wish-fulfilling. Sentient beings are more precious than a wish-fulfilling jewel because you can't practice morality, purify negative karma and achieve a higher rebirth with a wish-fulfilling jewel. Nor can you practice the three higher trainings and achieve the ultimate happiness of liberation or generate great compassion and achieve enlightenment with a wish-granting jewel, but you can with sentient beings. If you pray to a wish-granting jewel you can get a house, car, swimming pool and so on, but not higher rebirths, liberation and enlightenment. That's why sentient beings are most unbelievably precious. Which one is more precious; skies of wish-granting jewels or sentient beings? Sentient beings are more precious!

Therefore dedicating your life to others and helping them is the best, most exciting thing you can do. Serving them in any way you can and giving them whatever help you can give is what brings the most happiness. For example, by helping an old man carrying a very heavy load or by giving your seat to somebody in a bus, train or car. Doing whatever it is that sentient beings need, whether big or small, is the most satisfying, exciting thing you can do.

That's why making delicious food and offering it to the people that come here is a really great opportunity. Wow, wow, wow, wow. It is a way of offering comfort and happiness to sentient beings who are most wish-fulfilling. That's what brings the most happiness and excitement. It's the real Dharma. Dharma is something that protects your life, protects you from suffering and guides you to happiness. Therefore there is a great deal to rejoice in that you have this very precious opportunity to offer food to sentient beings that are most precious, dear, kind and wish-fulfilling.

PRACTICING BODHICITTA MINDFULNESS IN THE KITCHEN

Here are some ways to think while you are preparing and cooking the food.

When you are cutting anything, for example onions, think:

> *I am cutting the root of all sentient beings' suffering which comes from ignorance and the self-cherishing thought, with the knife of the wisdom realizing emptiness (shunyata) and bodhicitta.*

When you are washing pots and so on think:

> *I am washing away all the obscurations and negative karmas from all sentient beings minds.*

You can think that you are washing away your own obscurations and negative karmas but most important is to think you are washing away those of all sentient beings. And you can think the water is nectar coming from Vajrasattva, the Guru, His Holiness the Dalai Lama, or Guru Shakyamuni Buddha. There is always a lot of washing up to do in the kitchen and you can use the opportunity to purify all sentient beings' obscurations. It's very good if you can sincerely think this way because all the washing up becomes Dharma practice purifying your negative karma and defilements and collecting merits. In India even the beggars keep their pots very clean!

When you are sweeping the floor think that the broom is the whole path to enlightenment, especially wisdom and bodhicitta, and that the dust is all sentient beings' obscurations:

> *I am sweeping away the dust of all sentient beings' obscurations with the broom of the path to enlightenment and especially wisdom and bodhicitta.*

If you sincerely think this while you are cleaning it becomes real Dharma practice that benefits all sentient beings. In the lam rim it says to think that you are abandoning the dust of the three poisonous minds anger, attachment and ignorance—which are the gross obscurations and also the stains of the three poisonous minds, the subtle obscurations.

When you are kneading dough so that it can be made into any shape think:

> *I am taming all sentient beings minds by softening them with my two hands of the wisdom realizing emptiness and bodhicitta.*

When you are making momos or shapalep—rolling out pastry and filling it with cheese, potato and vegetables—think:

> *I am filling all sentient beings' minds with the realizations of the path from Guru devotion up to enlightenment so that they can actualize all the qualities of a Buddha.*

When you are cooking soup or other foods you can think that the fire is the Six Yogas' tummo fire that causes the kundalini to melt. Do the same meditation that is used to bless the inner offering in Highest Yoga Tantra. Or you can think that the fire is the wisdom realizing emptiness and the uncooked food is the unsubdued mind. By cooking the food all the gross and even the subtle delusions are purified and all the realizations of Buddha are achieved.

These are some ways of thinking as you are working in the kitchen. You can think in a similar way with other kitchen activities.

∞

Lama Zopa Rinpoche gave this advice at Tushita Meditation Centre, Dharamsala, India. Typed and edited by Ven. Sarah Thresher at Tushita, Dharamsala, 17 June 2013. Lightly edited by Claire Isitt, FPMT International Office, Oct 2013.

Lama Zopa Rinpoche is a Tibetan Buddhist scholar and meditator who for 30 years has overseen the spiritual activities of the extensive worldwide network of centers, projects and services that form the Foundation for the Preservation of the Mahayana Tradition (FPMT) which he founded with Lama Thubten Yeshe.

Vegetarian Menu Ideas

At VPI, lunch is our biggest meal of the day. According to the science of Eastern medicine, our digestive fire is highest at noontime, and thus we can process food most efficiently at this time. When on retreat, a large break is usually given after lunch to allow for time to digest the food, and again be energized and focused for spiritual practice. Dinner is simple, consisting of soup and salad, and keeping this meal light also supports our meditation. In fact, many monks and nuns choose to abstain from eating dinner altogether to keep the mind clear.

We've all heard the term, "balance" when referring to a healthy diet. Our bodies respond well when we eat a diet comprised of grains, protein, and vegetables – think of how challenging it would be to eat one of these groups by itself for even one week. Yet sometimes it can be hard to think up an entire meal which encompasses everything we need. With fast-paced, busy lifestyles, we often reach for what is quick and easy rather than what would be truly nourishing to our bodies.

Eating a balanced and wholesome diet is not impossible, even with a very full schedule – but it does take some planning ahead. For example, making a large portion of rice and then keeping it in the fridge to consume over a few days' time is a great way to always have a carbohydrate with your meals. Similarly, keeping cans of beans in your pantry will allow for protein to become a quick and simple addition to salads or stews. Joining a CSA (Community Supported Agriculture) can ensure that you always have new and fresh vegetables on hand.

Menus are wonderful ways to keep a concise and structured container for shopping, cooking, and eating. They also allow for us to try new and varied recipes. The grocery store can be an overwhelming place; where do we begin to shop? What are we hungry for? Instead of freshly asking ourselves this question each time we begin to push our shopping cart, we can brainstorm ahead of time healthy, delicious, and fun menus for the week.

The following menus are to serve as ideas or guides for planning a weekly meal schedule for yourself, your family, or your community. The intention behind listing these menus is to give a succinct conception of what a wholesome vegetarian lifestyle can look like – that it's not simply steamed kale and rice day after day. If we are not excited by the prospect of eating home-cooked food, we are much more likely to spend money in a restaurant or resort to snacking in place of a full meal.

A vegetarian lunch at VPI consists of a grain, protein, vegetable, and salad. Sweets are an optional and enjoyable addition. The following menus are lunch-specific, but can be used for dinner as well, as that is the time of day, understandably, that many people have the available time and resources to cook.

I will iterate as well that meals do not have to be compartmentalized – the grain does not need to be kept separate from the protein nor the vegetable. For example, a stew containing winter squash, kidney beans, and wild rice would contain all of the following meal components I have previously listed. Yet in the beginning, I find it becomes easier to think of a meal in its individual parts.

The recipes for most of the following menu items are to be found in this cookbook. Some items, such as "green salad" are not printed due to simplicity. Although these recipes are vegetarian in nature, you are welcome to add meat where you find necessary; though we do invite you to experiment with eating vegetarian sources of protein and observe the effect on your body and mind. You can find a more in-depth discussion of vegetarian protein sources in the section entitled "Vegetarian Protein." (page 67)

Whether you are cooking for yourself or others, we hope these menu ideas inspire you on your journey towards health and happiness.

∞

BROWN CORIANDER RICE (PG. 33)
ADZUKI BEANS (PG. 78)
BUTTERNUT SQUASH CURRY (PG. 46)
RAW KALE SALAD (PG. 105)

∞

WHITE CUMIN RICE (PG. 32)
CURRIED SWEET POTATO SOUP (PG. 97)
SPINACH SALAD (PG. 106)

∞

WHITE CUMIN RICE (PG. 32)
DELICATA SQUASH CASSEROLE (PG. 53)
BAKED LEMON GINGER TOFU (PG. 71)
ITALIAN SALAD (PG. 105)

∞

BUTTERNUT SQUASH PASTA WITH CARAMELIZED ONION, GARLIC, & SAGE (PG. 30)
DILLED AND SPICED GARBANZO BEANS (PG. 79)
ITALIAN SALAD (PG. 105)

∞

THE PERFECT BAKED POTATO (PG. 56)
TOPPED WITH CHEESE, SOUR CREAM, AND GREEN ONIONS
ADZUKI BEANS (PG. 78)
COLE SLAW (PG. 104)

∞

FALAFEL (PG. 77)
ZUCCHINI BABA GANOUSH (PG. 120)
SLICED TOMATOES
CURRIED SWEET POTATO SOUP (PG. 97)

∞

BROWN CORIANDER RICE (PG. 33)
MUSHROOMS AND TOMATOES (PG. 106)
TEMPEH AND KALE (PG.74)
GREEN SALAD

∞

∞

White Cumin Rice (pg. 32)
Lentil Patties and Sour Cream (pg. 82)
Roasted Kabocha Squash Moons (pg. 55)

∞

White Rice
Mung Bean Curry with Toasted Coconut (pg. 83)
Creamy Kabocha Squash (pg. 54)
Spinach Salad (pg. 106)

∞

Kasha with Almonds (pg. 38)
Roasted Beets (pg. 59)
Roasted Squash and Green Lentil Salad (pg. 73)
Cool Cucumber Yogurt Salad (pg. 107)

∞

Spinach Pesto Pasta (pg. 31)
Marinara Sauce (pg. 118)
Sweet Potato Layers (pg. 62)
Raw Kale Salad (pg. 105)

∞

Vegetable Enchiladas (pg. 60)
Mexican Rice (pg. 32)
Pico de Gallo (pg. 110)

∞

Coconut Basmati Rice (pg. 33)
Baked Lemon Ginger Tofu (pg. 71)
Butternut Squash Curry (pg. 46)

∞

Cooking with Love

by Venerable Tenzin Chogkyi

Sitting on the front deck of my yurt in Arizona, about two-thirds of the way through my first three-year retreat, I opened my meal bag – and then shut it immediately. I had had this experience many times in the last few weeks. It had nothing to do with the quality or freshness of the food, yet for some reason there was no way I was going to eat the lunch the caretakers had cooked for me!

Over a year later when I came out of retreat, I realized why: the two people who were working in the kitchen during that period of time were in conflict with each other; they cooked the food in stony silence with the occasional outburst of anger. I knew immediately that their toxic energy had been seeping into the food as surely as any other contaminant would have done.

I have noticed, especially when I've been in deep retreat, how important the energy that the cook brings to the meal is to its palatability and ability to nourish, as much as the nutritional value and the recipe… in fact, in my view, these qualities of the cook are far more important than those physical factors. Food cooked with love by people who understand and support what the meditators are doing is such an important component of a beneficial retreat experience – a factor often overlooked, or discounted completely, by those who have been indoctrinated by modern scientific reductionist thinking!

There is no doubt in my mind that we can subjectively experience food beyond its physicality; acutally perceiving the love and care behind the cook's intention. Many meditators have commented on this. So in addition to recipes, perhaps our cookbooks should also include loving-kindness, compassion and forgiveness meditations as well!

∞

Venerable Tenzin Chogkyi was ordained by His Holiness the Dalai Lama in 2004, and since 2006 has been teaching at various FPMT centers around the globe, in North and South America, India, Nepal, Australia, and New Zealand. She is a certified teacher of Cultivating Emotional Balance, a secular program in dealing with emotions developed by Allan Wallace and Paul Ekman, as well as a visiting teacher for the Liberation Prison Project having taught in prisons in the US, Colombia, Australia, and New Zealand. She served as the Director of Vajrapani Institute from 1992-1995.

GRAINS

Grains are a grounding aspect in a meal. As carbohydrates, they provide our bodies with energy needed for physical activity. By nature they are heavy and warm, and tend to be eaten more heartily in the colder, winter months. Cooking grains can be as simple as using a rice cooker to make a bowl of rice, or as elaborate as pressing your own pasta noodles. Whatever the method, grains are a staple product in any culture's cuisine, and are often found in the category of "comfort foods" – perhaps this is due to the familiar, grounding aspect that grains will bring to a meal.

Grains are good for all body types, and are especially essential for vegetarians, who can actually source some of their protein from grains. Eating an overabundance of grains can make us feel sluggish, bloated, and tired after meals. Eating too little grain can make us feel unsatisfied after meals.

Having a diet heavy in grain-consumption is good for those with more physically active lifestyles, as carbohydrates are a source of energy for our body and is needed for muscular movement. However, if your lifestyle involves a lot of sitting (like a desk job) and little movement, it is okay to have a lighter consumption of grain. You may find you have more energy this way.

Butternut Squash Pasta with Caramelized Onion, Garlic and Sage

For 1 lb. of pasta

1 butternut squash, peeled, seeded and cubed
2 medium onions, cut in thin half-moon slices
2-3 cloves of garlic, sliced

1 tbsp. powdered sage
1 bunch fresh parsley, chopped

Pre-heat oven to 425°.

Toss the butternut squash with olive oil, salt, and pepper and roast for 30-35 minutes, until cooked through. Turn halfway through cooking.

Cook the onions over low heat with a little bit of olive oil for at least 15 minutes. Do not salt the onions...this brings out the sweetness.

Remove 1/3 of the roasted squash and puree using a blender or food processor. Add a bit of hot water and the sage to blend. Then add salt and pepper to taste.

Cook pasta according to package instructions. When pasta is done, drain, and then fold in the pasta with the onion and butternut squash mixture.

In the same skillet that the onions were in, heat a little bit of oil and fry the garlic briefly, for 1 – 2 minutes, just until fragrant and a little browned. Don't burn it! Add this into the pasta along with the cubed butternut squash. Toss. Garnish with parsley.

Spinach Pesto Pasta

To make pesto (for 1 lb. of pasta):

1 lb. fresh spinach
1 bulb of garlic
1 small bunch fresh cilantro or basil
½ cup roasted walnuts
1 tsp salt

Juice of 1 lemon
¼ cup olive oil
½ cup shredded parmesan cheese
1½ cup whole milk

Pre-heat the oven to 400°. Cut the top off of your garlic bulb – the very top of each clove should be exposed. You can cover it with a light coat of oil or water or both; then wrap the bulb tightly with tinfoil and place it in the oven for 45 – 60 minutes. The cloves should be soft. Open the foil to let cool.

When garlic is cool enough to handle, squeeze out the roasted garlic and into a food processor.

Blanch the spinach: boil a pot of water with some salt, then add the spinach and stir. The spinach will wilt almost immediately. Turn off the heat, drain, and press the water out of the spinach as best you can.

Place spinach in a food processor (along with the garlic). Add the herbs, roasted nuts, salt, lemon juice, and olive oil. Blend well. (If you do not have a food processor, you should get one. In the meantime, you can chop the spinach, herbs, and nuts as fine as you can to a very, very fine consistency. Then add to a pot with the lemon juice, salt, and oil.)

Place the blended mixture into a saucepan over medium heat, along with the cheese and milk. Let the mixture come to a simmer, and heat for 15 minutes, stirring often to prevent sticking.

Cook pasta according to package instructions. Toss with pesto. Garnish with something pretty: cherry tomatoes, garbanzo beans, chopped parsley, or roasted broccoli florets.

31

Mexican Rice
Serves 4 – 6

2 cups of rice
1 tbsp. rice bran oil
2 garlic cloves, minced
1 8-oz can of tomato paste

3 ½ cups of water
1 tsp salt
1 bunch of fresh parsley, chopped

Heat oil in a saucepan and add the rice and garlic. Stirring often, sauté over medium heat for 5 – 10 minutes, or until the rice grains become solid white in color.

Add the tomato paste, water, and salt, stirring until paste dissolves. Bring mixture to a boil, cover, and reduce to a simmer over medium heat for 15 minutes. Once the rice is done, add the chopped parsley. Fluff with a fork before serving.

Cumin Rice
Serves 4 - 6

2 cups of jasmine white rice
1 tbsp. cumin seeds
1 tbsp. rice bran oil

1 yellow onion, chopped
3 ½ cups of water
1 tsp salt

Heat oil in a saucepan. Add the onion and cumin seeds and sauté, stirring often, for a couple minutes, or until seeds begin to pop. Add the rice, and continue to heat for 5 – 10 minutes, stirring often, until rice goes from being translucent to white in color.

At this point, add the water and salt and bring to a boil. Reduce to a simmer, cover, and cook for 15 minutes, or until all the water is absorbed. Fluff with a fork before serving.

Coconut Basmati Rice
Serves 2 – 3

1 cup white basmati rice
3 tbsp. dried flaked coconut
2 tsp coconut oil

1 ¾ cups of water
½ tsp salt

Heat oil in a saucepan. Add the coconut flakes and rice, and continue to heat for 5 – 10 minutes, stirring often, until rice goes from being translucent to white in color.

At this point, add the water and salt and bring to a boil. Reduce to a simmer, cover, and cook for 15 minutes, or until all the water is absorbed. Fluff with a fork before serving.

Brown Coriander Rice
Serves 2 – 3

1 cup short-grain brown rice
2 tbsp. coriander seeds, ground slightly
with mortar and pestle
2 tsp rice bran oil

Zest from 1 lemon
1 ¾ cups of water
½ tsp salt

Heat oil in a saucepan. Add the coriander seeds and rice, and continue to heat for 5 – 10 minutes, stirring often, until the seeds become very fragrant and the rice gets a little darker brown on the edges.

At this point, add the water, zest, and salt and bring to a boil. Reduce to a simmer, cover, and cook for 45 minutes, or until all the water is absorbed. Fluff with a fork before serving.

SWEET RICE
Serves 4

This rice is often made for special occasions in Tibetan culture.

2 cups white basmati rice
3 ½ cup water
1 tsp salt
2 tbsp. butter

¼ cup raisins or chopped dates
¼ cup almonds or cashews
¼ cup sugar or honey

Pre-heat oven to 350°. Toast the nuts in the oven by placing them on an ungreased baking sheet and cook for 15 minutes. Once toasted, chop them coarsely and set aside.

Melt the butter in a saucepan. Add the rice and toast briefly, then add the water, salt, and sugar, and bring to a boil. Reduce to a simmer and cover, cook for 15 minutes or until all the water is absorbed. Add the dried fruit and nuts in at the end. Fluff with a fork before serving.

BREAKFAST RICE PORRIDGE
Serves 2

2 cups cooked brown rice
¼ cup raisins
2 tbsp. almonds, chopped coarsely
1 tsp ground cardamom

½ tsp cinnamon
2 cups milk
1 cup water

Add all ingredients to a saucepan and bring to a boil. Simmer together, uncovered, until the rice begins to break down and some of the liquid evaporates, about 15-20 minutes. Add more liquid if necessary. Sweeten with honey if desired.

Vajrapani Granola
Makes about 8 cups

5 cups rolled oats
¼ cup dry flaked coconut
¼ cup sunflower seeds
½ cup almonds
¼ cup pumpkin seeds
2 tbsp. sesame seeds
1 tsp cinnamon
1 tsp cardamom

1 tsp powdered ginger
½ tsp nutmeg
½ tsp salt
¾ cup rice bran oil
½ cup agave nectar or honey
1 tbsp. molasses
½ tsp vanilla extract

Pre-heat oven to 300°. Grease a baking sheet well with rice bran oil.

In a saucepan, add the oil, sweetener, molasses, and vanilla. Warm over low heat and stir occasionally for about 3 minutes.

In a large bowl, combine all of the dry ingredients: the oats, coconut, seeds, nuts, spices, and salt. Toss together. Pour the warmed liquid mixture over the oats and stir together until fully coated. Spread out onto the baking sheet and bake for 40 minutes – make sure to take out 3 times during cooking to give the oats a quick toss so the ingredients will bake evenly.

Let cool completely before storing.

Simple Oatmeal
Serves 1

¾ cup rolled oats
1 ½ cups water
1 tsp cinnamon

Dash of salt
Splash of milk

Put oats, water, cinnamon, and salt into a saucepan. Bring to a boil and then reduce to a simmer for 7-10 minutes, stirring quite frequently.

Add a splash of milk near the end of cooking time. The oats should be broken down and mixture thick.

Drizzle with maple syrup for a sweet addition.

Optional add-ins:
· Blend 3 medjool dates with the water in a blender before cooking
· Cook with the oats a handful of raisins and ½ of an apple, chopped
· Toasted nuts or toasted coconut as a topping
· 1 tbsp. of peanut butter at the end of cooking, mix well to incorporate
· 1 tbsp. honey or molasses at the end of cooking

POLENTA PORRIDGE
Serves 4

1 cup polenta (yellow cornmeal)	*½ tsp salt*
4 cups water	*2 tbsp. butter (optional)*

Bring water and salt to a boil. Pour the polenta into the boiling water slowly, whisking as you do. Keep whisking together, every minute or so, until polenta begins to thicken. Cook uncovered, and stir every few minutes, cooking for a total of 20 minutes or more – depending upon your desired consistency. Cooking it for longer will create a creamier, softer finished product, rather than a coarse and textured porridge. Both ways are delicious.

Stir in the butter at the end of cooking if desired.

Ideas for leftover polenta:

· When refrigerated, polenta will harden to the form of its container. It's easy to handle and you can re-heat with a little bit of milk for breakfast porridge.

· Slice the polenta into thin rectangles and fry them in a little bit of olive oil, flipping once to brown and crisp both sides. Serve with vegetables on top and sprinkled with parmesan cheese.

MILLET

Serves 3 - 4

1 cup millet
2 ¼ cups water
½ tsp salt

½ tsp dried thyme
2 tbsp. butter (optional)

Toast millet in a saucepan for 10 minutes, stirring often. Add the water, salt, and thyme and bring to a boil. Cover and reduce to a simmer for 15 minutes, or until water is fully absorbed. Add butter at the end of cooking and fluff with a fork.

KASHA WITH ALMONDS

Serves 2 - 3

1 cup kasha
2 ¼ cups water
½ tsp salt

¼ cup almonds, crushed
and/or chopped well

Bring the water and salt to a boil in a saucepan. You must do this first before adding the kasha; otherwise you will end up with a porridge-like consistency. Kasha is a very good grain for breakfast porridge but that isn't what we are trying to do here.

Once the water comes to a boil, add the kasha and almonds, and bring back to a boil. Cover and simmer for 10 – 15 minutes, or until the water is fully absorbed.

Ten Tips for Mindful Eating
By Andrea Lieberstein

Mindful Eating enables us to enjoy our food more, and experience greater pleasure and nourishment from the food we eat. Through mindful awareness we become more attuned to our body's signals of pleasure, hunger and fullness. We can make choices that are most attuned to supporting our health and well-being. Learning and practicing mindfulness meditation regularly helps support the successful practice of mindful eating.

1) Take a Mini: Before eating a snack or meal, take a moment to breathe, pause, and notice any thoughts or feelings that may be present, particularly any in relation to the food you are about to eat. Notice how this may inform your choices of how much, when and what to eat, and desires or cravings for food. Use again as is helpful during eating a snack or meal.

2) Check into your hunger and fullness level before eating.

3) Feast your eyes visually on the food. Notice color, texture, shape.

4) Smell the food, noticing the nuances of smell with both nostrils.

5) Enjoy your food with all your senses. Notice any associations that arise whether pleasant or unpleasant.

6) Taste the food, first without chewing it. Noticing taste, texture, sensations... Then chew the food being as present as possible to fully savor and enjoy the experience. Swallow when ready.

7) Pay attention to the taste, noticing when taste is most strong, diminishes, enjoyment lessens etc., using this awareness to help inform decisions about how much, how little, when to stop, when to eat more, as is helpful.

8) Check into hunger and fullness levels before and occasionally throughout the snack or meal.

9) Take a moment to reflect upon how the food got to you, what went into making it, who and what was involved; people, sun, earth, water, farmers, etc.

10) Practice, practice, practice. At first we eat slowly when we practice mindful eating. The slow pace can be likened to the training wheels we use to learn to ride a bike. As we become more practiced and hone our attention skills, mindful eating becomes more natural. We can learn to eat mindfully not only slowly, but at different paces, settings, alone and with others. With attuned awareness we can eat in a way that becomes satisfying, guilt and struggle free, and with the quantities and quality that support our optimum health and well-being.

Learning and having a regular practice of mindfulness meditation helps support and deepen your practice of mindful eating.

Bon Appetit!

∞

Andrea Lieberstein, MPH, RD, RYT © 2014 Mindfulness-Based Eating Awareness Training and Coaching, Mindful Eating Programs for the General Public and Health Professionals
alieberstein@gmail.com - www.mindfuleatingtraining.com

VEGETABLE DISHES

Vegetables are nutrient-dense foods, meaning that they are full of things that are good for you, while packed into a low amount of calories. Varying vegetable consumption to include many types of colors and qualities ensures that we ingest a range of nutrients necessary to support our health. A simple yet profound fact is that vegetables of certain colors tend to contain certain kinds of vitamins and minerals. So experimenting with different vegetables in cooking is not only an easy way to be creative in the kitchen, but also a way to get a wide range of nutrients. Every vegetable is not for everyone, but you can experiment with different seasonings and cooking methods that may hook your taste buds.

Vegetables are living entities. It always amazes me that naturally a plant will reach its leaves up towards the sun, and respond to other cues in the environment as well. As humans, we are also living entities, which respond well to eating this food that is alive and thriving, always growing and changing. For me, it reminds me that I am always growing and changing too. It reminds me that I also respond to my environment, and thrive and grow when the conditions are right. Vegetables serve as great reminders that no matter how intellectually brilliant our minds are, our bodies have an incredible wealth of wisdom too.

The types of vegetables we eat also vary and fluctuate with the seasons. Certain vegetables that grow in abundance during the summer are usually foods that we crave and work well with our bodies during that time. These foods tend to be lighter, crisper, and colder in nature. Things like zucchini, summer squash, tomatoes, lettuce, greens, and fruit, are eaten in abundance during this time. Likewise, in the winter, we tend to eat foods which are heartier, heavier, thicker, and warmer. Some examples of these are winter squash, potatoes, and beets. Sometimes there are preparation methods that tend to be seasonal as well. Raw vegetables and fruits are often taken more in the summer. Cooking and stewing is more common in the winter.

Located in California, at VPI we have access to most foods all year round, sometimes it's hard to remember what seasonal eating looks like. We can usually tell what the seasonal foods are based on whether the price is high or low for that food in the grocery store. We may also find that in listening to our bodies, our cravings may actually guide us toward seasonal eating. We may notice, for example, that eating a crunchy cucumber salad in the middle of January doesn't feel as nurturing as a bowl of steaming puréed squash soup.

We are faced with many choices when shopping for our food – organic or non-organic; GMO or non-GMO; Local or far; Family farmed or factory farmed? I'd like to explore some of those choices and offer information that can help you make informed decisions.

Buying organic foods not only can be a choice to support our health, but likewise a decision we make in order to support organic farming methods. Each time we buy organic in the grocery store, we are exercising our power to support the organic foods movement. However, we may be torn by the price differences between organic and non-organic produce; eating organic may not always be financially feasible. When working within a budget, sometimes a balance must be reached between eating a combination of organic and conventional produce.

The following lists of produce – "dirty dozen" and "clean fifteen" – are guides to decide which foods to buy as organic and which to buy as conventional. Produce classified as the "dirty dozen" are foods which you should always buy organic, if you can manage, because of the heavy use of pesticides on the food. It's even argued that it may be best to either buy these foods organic or not buy them at all, because of the unknown health risks posed by ingesting residual pesticides.

The next category of produce is, for all intents and purposes, safe for consumption whether organic or conventional. Pesticide usage may be less on these foods, or they may possess a shell or thick skin which protects the inside fruit from absorbing harmful chemicals. Of course, if you'd like to support the organic farming movement, by all means please do purchase organic when possible.

Dirty Dozen: Apples, Strawberries, Grapes, Celery, Peaches, Spinach, Sweet Bell Peppers, Nectarines, Cucumbers, Cherry Tomatoes, Snap Peas, and Potatoes

Clean Fifteen: Avocados, Sweet Corn, Pineapples, Cabbage, Sweet Peas, Onions, Asparagus, Mangoes, Papayas, Kiwi, Eggplant, Grapefruit, Cantaloupe, Cauliflower, Sweet Potatoes

There's also the debate of genetically modified foods (GMO) versus non-GMO foods. The molecular structure of GMO crops is altered to be pesticide-resistant. America is the largest producer of GMO foods, and the most popular GMO foods that grow in America are soy and corn. The United States Government deems GMO foods safe to eat; however, many people are wary about eating GMOs, for fear that their negative health impacts are more long-term in nature, and that we haven't had the proper longitudinal studies to get accurate results. As a continent, Europe decided to ban GMO foods. Some people choose not to eat GMO foods so as not to support companies like Monsanto, who not only create GMO crops, but patent them, and then sue small farms for patent-infringement when GMO seeds are found on the small farmer's land.

GMO corn and soy aren't limited to cobs of corn and packages of tofu; lots of foods on the shelves of the grocery store contain corn in the form of high fructose corn syrup. Likewise, soy is used as a filler in many frozen vegetarian protein alternatives, and also an emulsifier, called "soy lecithin," which you can find added to many products ranging from tea bags to salad dressings. Buying organic products that contain corn and soy, such as corn flakes and miso, ensure that they are GMO-free.

Many of us do not grow our own produce, and thus we have many choices to make about the farming practices we'd like to support when we go to the grocery store or farmer's market. These are exciting choices involving our ethics and financial practicality. The following recipes are ways to celebrate vegetables, and pay homage to the cycle of planting, growing, and harvesting that brings them to our tables.

Tofu Vegetable Curry
Serves 3 - 4

1 package of firm tofu, cubed	*½ head cauliflower, chopped*
Rice Oil	*1 14-ounce can of coconut milk*
Bragg's Liquid Aminos or soy sauce	*4 tomatoes, chopped*
1 tbsp. coconut oil	*1 8-ounce can of tomato paste*
1 onion, chopped	*¼ cup peanut butter*
1 jalapeno, chopped	*½ tsp turmeric*
1 tbsp. ginger, chopped	*1 tsp coriander*
¼ head green cabbage, cut into squares	*½ tsp salt*
1 sweet potato, cubed	*2 cups water*

Drain tofu and pat dry. Cut into small cubes and then add to a frying pan with a little bit of rice oil and some Bragg's Liquid Aminos or soy sauce. Heat together over medium flame for 15-20 minutes and stir every now and then. All the liquid from the tofu should evaporate and the cubes should become slightly browned on the outside and a little more firm.

Either in a blender or with a whisk, blend together the coconut milk, tomato paste, water, peanut butter, and spices.

Heat coconut oil in a saucepan. Add the onion and cook for 10 minutes. Then add the jalapenos and ginger, and sauté for 2 more minutes, stirring often. Add the tomatoes and the paste mixture. Stir together and bring to a boil. Now add the cabbage, potatoes, and cauliflower. Reduce to a simmer and cover. Let this cook together for 30 minutes. Add the tofu and serve.

BUTTERNUT SQUASH CURRY

Serves 6

1 yellow onion, chopped
1 large or 2 small butternut squash, peeled and cubed
1 jalapeno, minced
1 tbsp. fresh grated ginger
2 cloves garlic, minced
½ tsp turmeric

½ tsp mustard powder
1 tsp cumin
1 tsp coriander
2 14-oz cans coconut milk
1 cup water
1 bunch basil, julienned
Salt and pepper to taste

Sauté the onion for 10 minutes in a little bit of oil. Add the jalapeno, ginger, and garlic, stirring often, and cook for another 2 minutes. Add the spices along with a splash of water to moisten them. Then add the squash, coconut milk, water, and a sprinkle of salt and pepper. Bring to a boil, then reduce to a gentle simmer for 15 minutes, or until squash is cooked through. Stir in the basil before serving.

Coconut Cabbage
Serves 6

1 large head of green cabbage
3 tbsp. coconut oil
½ tsp salt

1 14-ounce can of coconut milk
1 bunch fresh parsley
Cut cabbage into 1" squares.

Heat coconut oil in a saucepan over medium heat. Add cabbage and salt, and stir to coat with oil. Add a few tablespoons of the coconut milk, cover, and simmer for 30 minutes. Stir occasionally.

Add remaining coconut milk and parsley, and cook together for 10 minutes.

Spicy Cabbage
Serves 6

1 head of green cabbage, sliced thinly
1 tbsp. rice bran oil
1 or 2 jalapenos, minced
2 cloves garlic, minced
1 tbsp. fresh ginger, chopped

2 tbsp. soy sauce or
Bragg's Liquid Aminos
½ tsp salt
½ tsp red chili flakes
1 tsp sesame oil

Heat rice oil in a saucepan. Add the jalapenos, garlic, and ginger and heat for 1 minute or so. Add the cabbage, soy sauce or Bragg's, and the salt. Stir and cook over high heat for 10-15 minutes; cabbage will be cooked but a little crunchy. Stir in the red chili flakes and drizzle with sesame oil before serving.

CURRIED COCONUT CARROTS AND GARBANZO BEANS
Serves 3 - 4

*8 large carrots, peeled, and sliced
diagonally into 1" rounds
1 red onion, chopped
1 jalapeno, chopped
2 cloves garlic, minced
1 tbsp. fresh ginger, chopped
1 tbsp. coconut oil*

*2 14-oz cans coconut milk
1 can garbanzo beans
1 tsp turmeric
1 tsp powdered coriander
1 small bunch fresh cilantro, chopped
Salt and pepper to taste
(optional) 1 package of firm tofu

Heat coconut oil in a pan. Add the onion and cook for 10 minutes. Then add the jalapenos, ginger, and garlic. Sauté for 2 more minutes, stirring often. Add the carrots, turmeric, and coriander. Stir together briefly. Now add the coconut milk and garbanzo beans, cover, and simmer together for 15 minutes, until carrots are cooked but still firm. Add salt and pepper to taste, and the fresh cilantro before serving.

*Optional: Cube tofu and fry separately. Add in the tofu with the cilantro.

CARROTS WITH BUTTER
Serves 4

*6 – 8 carrots, peeled and sliced into ½"
rounds
4 tbsp. butter
1 yellow onion, sliced into half-moons*

*1 tbsp. honey + ½ cup hot water
½ tsp allspice
Salt and pepper
1 small bunch fresh parsley, chopped*

Heat the butter in a saucepan and add the onions. Cook over low heat for 10 minutes. Add the carrots, honey/water mixture, allspice, salt, and pepper. Heat ingredients for another 15 minutes until carrots are soft. Garnish with chopped parsley.

CARROTS WITH CINNAMON
Serves 2

4 carrots
1 tsp coconut oil
¼ cup raisins

1 tsp cinnamon
3 tbsp. water or coconut milk
Drizzle of honey (optional)

Cut carrots in half length-wise, then again, to create long spears. Heat the oil in a saucepan. Add the carrots and sauté over medium high heat for 5-10 minutes. The carrots should brown on some of the sides and be cooked but still firm. Add the raisins, cinnamon, and water or milk. Stir, and then cover to steam for another 3 minutes or so.

Before serving, you can drizzle with honey.

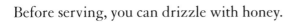

MASHED CAULIFLOWER WITH TAHINI AND PEAS
Serves 4

1 head cauliflower
½ cup coconut milk
4 tbsp. coconut oil or butter
½ cup tahini
1 tsp salt

2 tsp dried thyme
3 cloves fresh garlic, minced
1 small package frozen peas
½ cup parmesan cheese (optional)

Pre-heat oven to 350°.

Chop the cauliflower and place in cooking pot. Cover the cauliflower with water and bring to a boil; simmer for 20 minutes, or until cauliflower is completely tender. Drain and add to a large bowl. In large bowl, add the coconut milk, oil or butter, tahini, salt, thyme, and garlic. Mash the mixture well with a potato masher. Stir in the peas. Put into a baking dish and cover tightly; then bake for 15 minutes. If using, uncover and sprinkle with parmesan cheese. Put back in the oven for 5 minutes.

Roasted Tahini Coated Cauliflower
Serves 4

2 small or 1 large head of cauliflower	*¼ cup warm (not hot) water*
¼ cup tahini	*2 tsp curry powder*
¼ cup olive oil	*Salt and pepper*

Pre-heat oven to 375°.

Stir together the tahini and warm water. Do this by adding the water slowly and whisking as you go. Tahini can curdle if you heat it too fast. Then stir in the olive oil, curry powder, salt and pepper.

Chop cauliflower florets into bite-size pieces. Toss the cauliflower with the tahini mixture until all pieces are coated. Spread evenly onto the baking sheet and cook for 20-25 minutes.

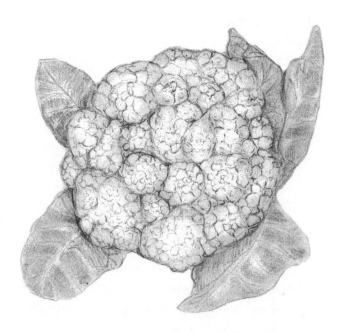

Cauliflower and Potato (Aloo Ghobi)
Serves 6

1 head of cauliflower, chopped	½ tsp cinnamon
4 russet potatoes	1 tsp coriander
1 tbsp. rice bran oil	3 cloves garlic, minced
1 yellow onion, chopped	1 tbsp. fresh ginger, chopped
1 tbsp. cumin seeds	½ cup water
1 tsp mustard seeds	Salt to taste

Wash the potatoes well and then slice them into thick rounds. Add them to a pot of water with some salt and bring to a boil. Reduce to a simmer and cook for 10 minutes, or until potatoes are almost fully cooked. Drain, and run cool water over them to stop from cooking. Then cut them into cubes and set aside.

Heat oil in a pan and then add the onions, cumin seeds, and mustard seeds. Heat until the seeds begin to pop. Add the garlic, ginger, cinnamon, and coriander, and water, and stir briefly to make a sort of chunky paste. Stir in the cauliflower and cook over medium-high heat, stirring often, until they begin to get soft. Add the other ¼ cup water and cover to steam them a few minutes. Add in the potatoes and cook, uncovered, for another 10 minutes. Add salt to taste.

CROOKNECK SQUASH AND CORN IN ANCHO CHILI SALSA
Serves 4

4 yellow crookneck squash, chopped
Kernels from 1 ear of fresh corn
½ cup of sour cream (optional)

For the salsa:
2 dry ancho chilies
4 tomatoes, diced

2 garlic cloves, diced
1 onion, diced
1 bunch of cilantro
Salt and pepper
3 cups water
1 8-ounce can of tomato paste

Boil a small amount of water and set aside.

Over an open flame and using tongs, heat the ancho chilies one at a time until they become smoked – about 20 – 30 seconds in direct flame. If you have an electric stove-top, you can always fry the chilies in a frying pan.

After you smoke the chilies, soak the chilies in the hot water for a few minutes to soften them.

In a blender, combine the chilies (and their soaking water), tomatoes, garlic, onion, and cilantro. Blend well. Add the mixture to a saucepan along with the 3 cups of water, tomatoes paste, and bring to a boil.

Simmer for a few minutes before adding the squash and corn, then simmer together for 7 – 10 minutes, or until yellow crookneck squash are cooked. Taste for salt and pepper. If using, stir in the sour cream before serving.

Delicata Squash Casserole
Serves 4

3 delicata squash, no need to peel
4 cloves garlic, minced
¼ cup olive oil
1 onion, sliced into half moons
1 cup cheese – ½ cup parmesan and ½ cup
swiss

½ cup milk
4 tbsp. butter
Salt and pepper

Pre-heat oven to 375°.

Cut squash in half and scoop out the seeds. Slice into thin half moons. Add them to a large bowl and along with the olive oil, salt, pepper, and garlic. Toss to coat.

Have ready the sliced onions, grated cheese, and the sliced squash. In your baking pan, place a layer of squash, then a layer of onions, then a cheese layer. Repeat this twice. Finally pour the milk over the top and slice the butter, placing the squares atop the last layer. Cover tightly with tinfoil and bake for 35 – 40 minutes. Test to see if they are done by poking squash with a fork. The squash should be very soft and turn a deeper orange color.

Turn any leftovers into a dip by blending it in a food processor or blender. You may have to add a little more milk – but try without first.

CREAMY KABOCHA SQUASH
Serves 4

2 tbsp. coconut oil
1 large or 2 small kabocha squash, peeled,
de-seeded and cut into 1" cubes
1 tbsp. fresh ginger, minced
2 cloves garlic, sliced
½ tsp turmeric

1 tsp coriander
1 14-oz can coconut milk
1 bunch fresh cilantro, chopped
1 package frozen peas

Heat coconut oil in a saucepan until melted. Add the ginger and garlic, and stir briefly over low heat taking care not to burn. Once they smell fragrant, add the squash, turmeric, coriander, and about 1 cup of coconut milk. Keep heating over medium-low heat and stir to prevent sticking. Cook for about 7 minutes, then add another splash of coconut milk, stir, and heat. Continue this process for 30-40 minutes, until all the coconut milk is used up. If you need more moisture you can add splashes of water, too. Add the peas and cilantro and turn off heat; but keep covered for at least 3 minutes, so that the peas cook through before serving.

Roasted Kabocha Squash Moons
Serves 2 - 4

1 kabocha squash	*1 tsp dried thyme*
¼ cup olive oil	*½ tsp cinnamon*
1 tsp salt	*3 tbsp. brown sugar*
½ tsp pepper	

Pre-heat oven to 375°. Oil a baking sheet or put down parchment paper.

Cut the kabocha squash in half and scoop out the seeds. Peel the squash halves as best you can – they can be tricky – but it's okay if some of the skin is still present. Put the squash cut-face down on the cutting board and slice into wedges, like pieces of an orange.

In a bowl, toss the squash with olive oil, salt, pepper, thyme, cinnamon, and sugar. Make sure all the squash is coated with oil.

Place the squash moons onto the baking sheet and roast for 45 – 60 minutes. Check on the squash halfway through and flip them over.

THE BEST BAKED POTATO
Serves 1

1 russet potato, washed well
¼ cup of olive oil
Pinch of salt

Pre-heat oven to 350°. Cut the potato in half length-wise. Put the olive oil and salt together in small bowl. Roll the potato halves in the olive oil and place face-down on a baking sheet. (No need to grease the baking sheet). Add a splash of water to the pan as well. Cook in the oven for 30 minutes, or until potato is soft when poked with a fork.

Optional Toppings:

. Tomato Sauce
. Vegetarian Chili
. Sour Cream
. Cottage Cheese
. Fresh Cilantro or Parsley

. Green Onions
. Shredded Cheese
. Chopped Olives
. Chopped Tomatoes
. Butter

Sweet Potato Millet Patties
Serves 4 - 6 people (Makes about 12 patties)

2 lbs. (about 4 large) sweet potatoes
1 cup millet
1 yellow onion, chopped
3 cloves garlic, minced

1 tbsp. powdered cumin
1 bunch fresh cilantro, chopped
Salt and pepper

Pre-heat oven to 350°. Place parchment paper on a baking sheet, or grease it very lightly with olive oil.

Wash the sweet potatoes well. Cut into slices and boil them for 10 minutes or until soft. Drain.

Cook the millet: bring 2.5 cups of water and some salt to a boil, then add the millet, and simmer while covered for 15-20 minutes, or until the water is fully absorbed.

Add all ingredients to a bowl: the cooked sweet potatoes, cooked millet, onion, garlic, and spices. Mash the mixture together using a potato masher; it will stick together and be very goopy.

Drop the 'dough' in large scoops onto the baking sheet (about ½ cup per patty) and flatten with the back of a spoon. Bake for 30-40 minutes, flipping the patties halfway through.

Sweet Potato Pie
Serves 4 - 6

2 lbs. (about 4 large) sweet potatoes, peeled and cut into chunks

½ cup milk

4 tbsp. butter or coconut oil

1 tsp cinnamon

3 tbsp. olive oil

1 onion, chopped

3 cloves garlic, minced

2 tbsp. dried thyme

1 tbsp. dried oregano

2 tsp paprika

1 lb. mushrooms, sliced

3 carrots, peeled and chopped

3 stalks celery, halved lengthwise and chopped

3 tomatoes, chopped

1 cup water

1 cup frozen green peas

3 tbsp. all-purpose flour (or chickpea flour)

3 tbsp. tamari (or Bragg's Liquid Aminos)

½ cup shredded parmesan cheese (optional)

Preheat oven to 350°.

Mash sweet potatoes: Peel sweet potatoes and cut them into large rounds. Add them to a saucepan with enough water to cover and a bit of salt. Bring them to a boil and simmer for 20 minutes. Drain. Return to the saucepan and add the milk, butter or oil, cinnamon, and salt. Mash together.

Sautée vegetables: In a skillet, heat olive oil and add onions, cook them for 10 minutes. Then add the garlic, cook for 1 minute, and then the spices and water, stir to dissolve spices. Add the mushrooms, carrots, celery, tomatoes, cover, and cook for 10 minutes.

Create the thickener: Dissolve the flour by adding a small amount of hot water and stirring with a fork or whisk until all the lumps are gone. Add this, the peas, and tamari to the vegetable mixture and stir well. Cook for another minute. The mixture should become a little thicker.

Assemble: Pour vegetable mixture into a 9x13" baking dish. On top, layer the mashed sweet potatoes and sprinkle with parmesan cheese. Bake for 30-35 minutes.

Simple Roasted Beets
Serves 4

1 lb. (about 5) red beets
¼ cup olive oil

¼ cup water
Salt

Pre-heat oven to 400°. Peel and cube the beets and add them to a small baking dish. Drizzle the olive oil and water over the beets, then add a dash of salt. Shake pan back and forth to coat. Cover tightly with tinfoil and bake for at least 40 minutes. Check them to see if they are done by poking them with a fork; the beets should be easily pierced but still somewhat firm. Be careful not to overcook them.

Beets with Sour Cream
Serves 4

1 lb. (about 5) beets
3 tbsp. olive oil
¼ cup water
1 tsp sesame oil

½ tsp mustard powder
1 tsp dried dill
1 cup sour cream

Cook beets according to the previous recipe "Simple Roasted Beets," using the olive oil and water.

Remove beets from the oven and drain off most of the liquid. Let cool. Add the sesame oil, mustard powder, dill, and sour cream. Refrigerate and serve cold.

Vegetable Enchiladas
Serves 4

To Make Salsa:
6 beefsteak tomatoes
3 garlic cloves
1 onion, chopped
1 or 2 jalapeno peppers
(de-seed them to make it less spicy)
¼ cup water
½ bunch fresh cilantro

To Make Enchiladas:
3 carrots, sliced into 1" rounds
2 russet potatoes cut into small cubes
2 cups cooked black or pinto beans
1 cup of shredded cheese
Sour cream
1 bunch of chopped green onions
12 corn tortillas

Pre-heat oven 325°.

First make the salsa: Using a blender, blend the tomatoes with the onion, garlic, pepper, cilantro, and water. Add salt and pepper to taste. Pour the mixture into a saucepan and bring to a boil. Simmer for 10 minutes, then turn off heat and set aside.

In a separate saucepan, add the carrots and potatoes. Cover with water and bring to a boil, simmer and stir often for about 12 minutes. They should be almost cooked but not overcooked. Strain and run cool water over them to stop them from cooking more.

Now to assemble the enchiladas: Put a little oil in the bottom of a baking dish. Warm up the corn tortillas 2 at a time in a frying pan. This allows you to bend them without breaking.

Once the tortillas are warm, stuff them one at a time with the cooked carrots, potatoes, and beans. Fold the stuffed tortilla in half and place it in the baking pan; drizzle some salsa inside. Repeat this process with all the tortillas so that they are side-by-side in the baking dish. Pour over top the rest of the salsa, and then sprinkle with shredded cheese and green onion. Put in the oven for 15-20 minutes, or until potatoes are finished cooking and the cheese is melted on top. Finally, dollop with sour cream, as desired.

Stuffed Zucchini
Serves 4

4 medium zucchinis
¼ cup olive oil
2 tbsp. coconut oil or butter
1 onion, chopped
4 cloves garlic, minced
½ cup cooked brown rice
(leftover works great!)

4 ounces of tomato paste
1 tsp dried oregano
1 tsp chili powder
Salt and pepper
4 ounces goat cheese
¼ cup parmesan cheese

Pre-heat oven to 350°. Grease a baking sheet, or line with parchment paper.

Slice zucchinis in half and scoop out the insides into a bowl and set it aside. Toss the hollowed zucchinis with the olive oil and salt and place them face-up onto baking sheet.

Heat the coconut oil or butter in a saucepan and add the onions and garlic, then sauté over medium heat until the onions begin to turn translucent, about 10 minutes. Add the zucchini insides, brown rice, tomato paste, and spices. Cook together, stirring, for another 5 minutes. Remove from heat and stir in the cheeses.

Spoon the filling into the zucchini shells. Bake for 30 – 35 minutes.

Sweet Potato Layers

Makes one 11x13" baking dish

2 lbs sweet potatoes	*1 tbsp coriander seeds*
1 ½ lbs zucchini	*Olive oil*
2 onions, chopped	*1 cup nutritional yeast*
4 cloves garlic, sliced very thin	*1 ½ cups coconut milk*

Pre-heat oven to 400°. Lightly grease the bottom of a baking dish.

Cut the ends off the zucchini and then cut the zucchinis in half. Stand them up on the flat part of the zucchini and slice them very, very thin this way. Add them to a bowl and toss with olive oil, salt, and pepper.

Peel the sweet potatoes. Do the same as the zucchini to slice them very, very thin, and again, add them to a bowl and toss them with olive oil, salt, and pepper.

Heat a couple tbsp of olive oil in a frying pan. Add the onions, garlic, and coriander seeds, and cook over low heat for 10 minutes until onions are translucent and all is fragrant.

Whisk together nutritional yeast and coconut milk.

Now, to assemble! Using half of the sweet potatoes, layer them in the bottom of the pan. Follow by using all of the zucchini, then spread the onion mixture on top, then add one more layer of sweet potatoes. Pour over the nutritional yeast/coconut milk mixture. Cover tightly with tinfoil and bake for 40 - 60 minutes, or until sweet potatoes are cooked (check by poking with a fork).

Rejoice Before You Eat
By Nina Tomkiewicz

I am always amazed when I consciously remind myself of the plethora of food I have available to me. Persimmons, kale, squash; prepared in the oven, on the stove, steamed, sautéed, baked, or fried. Ingredient combinations and cooking methods are vast in this day and age, yet instead of constantly rejoicing at the mere fact that I get to be creative with my food choices, I become stuck on liking "this not that," or "this flavor not that flavor." I worry about whether the amount of food will be enough or too little. I spend time debating over whether I want wheat or rye, tofu or tempeh, tea or coffee. I circle the grocery store, ill-stricken that the coconut milk is out of stock. I realize that there's a difference between being in touch with my preferences and becoming attached to them!

When we equate happiness with acquiring our favorite foods, a true joy that comes with eating is glossed over. Likewise, the way we eat has transformed from a ritualistic practice into a hurried activity, and we miss a lot of opportunities to rejoice in these rushed moments. As demonstrated by the advent of fast food restaurants, when we eat we are taking less time to connect with others as well as our food. Time for meals has been deemed unimportant in the face of productivity, work, and an on-the-go lifestyle. This mindset contributes to feelings of dissatisfaction, and creates blockages to truly feeling nourished after a meal. There is much more to eating than the mere food itself: the preparation, the anticipation, the feeling of hunger abating, connecting with others, connecting with the food, and connecting with ourselves.

Taking the time to pause, reflect, and rejoice before eating allows us to recognize the wonderful opportunity we have to satisfy our bodies in this way. We can recognize the gift of sharing a meal, and how amazing it is that we can experiment with our food. Even if we didn't cook the meal in our own kitchen, and are being served in a restaurant, we can still take a moment to put our mind in a grateful space. During these quiet moments of reflection, we can think about several things:

1. All the causes and conditions that brought the food to you, in this moment, ready to eat. There are many people who planted, tended to, and harvested the food. As the food was being grown, it was given water and sunlight; it was part of an ecosystem that allowed it to flourish. Then there were the people who transported the food to the store or restaurant, and finally those who prepared it. All of this happened so that you could enjoy and be nourished in this moment.

2. We can think about how lucky we are to live in a time where food is available to us. Eating is a basic need, and not having to worry about where our next meal is coming from is a huge blessing. We can have gratitude for this.

3. Imagine offering the food to your Guru, a higher power, God, or any of your teachers or guides. The act of offering in general is a means of cutting through miserliness, and opening up our generosity. When we are in the presence of a delicious meal, we can imagine offering this wonderfully prepared food to all those forces in our life that give rise to such fortunate circumstances.

4. Imagine sharing the food with those who do not have food. You can imagine, that sitting at your table with you are people who are hungry and need food. You can imagine sharing with them the nourishment that you have, and as you satisfy your hunger you will also satisfy the hunger of other beings.

5. Think, "I am going to consume this food for the benefit of others. I am going to nourish myself so that I give my body what it needs to be healthy. By taking care of myself this way, I will be able to live fully and help other beings to my fullest potential." It is beneficial to think of others whenever possible; this is the Bodhicitta motivation.

∞

Nina Tomkiewicz served as the Kitchen Manager and Cook at Vajrapani Institute from April 2014 to August 2015. Before leaving to pursue a degree in Social Work, she compiled this cookbook for Vajrapani community and patrons to enjoy.

Blessing the food with your Body, Speech, and Mind

OM AH HUM (3 times)

∞

Offering Prayer

La ma sang gya la ma chho
De zhin la ma ge dun te
Kun gyi je po la ma te
La ma nam la chho par bul

The guru is Buddha, the guru is Dharma
The guru is Sangha also
The guru is the creator of all (happiness)
To all gurus, I make this offering

May this food nourish me, so that I may nourish others.

∞

Vegetarian Protein

A vegetarian lifestyle is admittedly not for everyone; however, it's impossible to ignore the plethora of health and environmental benefits that ensue from eliminating meat from our diets. Not only has it been shown that excessive red meat and dairy consumption directly correlate to the prominence of cancer and heart disease, but the practice of farming of cows contributes largely to the pollution of green house gas emissions. While many of find meat an important addition to our diets in order to maintain strength, energy, and overall well-being, it may be possible to cut down on our meat consumption as a whole, thereby reducing the pressure on animals who sacrifice their lives to provide us with a protein source.

As per the advice of his doctors, the Dalai Lama even eats meat for the sake of his health. Yet he strongly advises everyone who has the opportunity and means to be vegetarian to do so – though we are not physically killing the animals ourselves, there is an aspect of animal welfare that is being harmed by the demands we place upon our grocery stores, restaurants, and food providers for meat products.

Reducing our meat consumption is no easy feat, yet actively deciding to consume less meat gives us the opportunity to practice mindfulness in our day-to-day eating habits. What happens when we go out for breakfast and our first impulse is to order a side of bacon? Or if we are perusing the grocery store and imagining a roast chicken as our dinner that evening? Instead of allowing ourselves to indulge in a meat product, perhaps we can alter our mental perspective and dwell in a state of compassion for all the animals; then we can sacrifice our sense of pleasure as a gesture to them.

And by "sacrifice our pleasure," I do not mean that we refrain from having protein in our meal that evening! In fact, it would be harmful to deprive ourselves of the nutrients we need to have energy and vitality in our lives. What I mean is that perhaps we can change our perspective on what it means to get an adequate amount of protein in our diet, and thereby learn a truth that sees beyond our habitual response to hunger. Perhaps our well-being and health doesn't rely upon us eating meat every day, and instead we can learn to include other foods, such as legumes, nuts, seeds, and beans, into our diet to achieve adequate health.

So how do we get an adequate amount of protein in our diets if we aren't consuming meat on a daily basis?

There are plenty of other foods that contain protein. In fact, even vegetables contain protein! (However, you'd have to eat about 7 cups of leafy greens to get the same amount of protein as one portion of beef provides.) See the table below as a protein guideline:

Beef (1/4 lb): 36 g	Miso (per cup): 32 g
Chicken (1/4 lb): 30g	Lentils (per cup): 18g
Tuna (1/4 lb): 26g	Leafy Greens (per cup): 5g
Tofu (per cup): 21g	Quinoa (1 cup): 8g
Eggs (2): 12g	Kasha (1 cup): 6g
Black Beans (per cup): 15g	Nuts/Seeds (1/2 cup): 30g
Chickpeas (per cup): 15g	Yogurt, Plain (1 cup): 9g
Adzuki Beans (per cup): 17g	

As advised by the Centers for Disease Control and Prevention, women should eat around 46 grams of protein per day, and men around 56 grams of protein per day. Using this chart, you can see that achieving this goal is made simple by including a protein source with every meal. For example, having almonds with your breakfast, beans with lunch, and miso for dinner.

Using this table as a guideline, getting adequate protein in our diet is entirely possible with the addition of little or no meat. Of course, we must take body type and lifestyle into account in order to assess what a state of health looks like – every body has slightly different needs. However, it remains beneficial to keep in mind that your protein-need can be satisfied while abstaining from meat. You may, however, need to be more creative, more inclusive, and reach beyond the Standard American Diet we all grew up with to do so.

Every recipe in this book can be seen as a gateway into the vastness of vegetarian cooking, which admittedly is a paradigm shift away from the aforementioned Standard American Diet, advising us to eat 15% of our daily diet in protein – approximately 75 grams of protein per day! No wonder we feel as though we are never getting enough... It takes intention to choose not to eat meat, and these recipes can provide alternative meal choices when you are unsure how to structure your protein intake in a healthy way. Each time that you do, rejoice that you are choosing to lower the demand for meat in this country, which can potentially have a huge, positive impact on the livelihood of animals as well as our world at large.

CABBAGE AND CHICKPEAS
Serves 3 - 4

3 tbsp. butter or olive oil
1 onion, chopped
2 cloves garlic, minced
1 tbsp. coriander seeds
3 carrots, shredded

½ head of (large) green cabbage,
sliced thin
2 cups (about 1 can) cooked chickpeas
2 tbsp. apple cider vinegar
½ cup water

Heat butter or oil in a heavy bottomed skillet. Add the onion, garlic, and coriander seeds and mix briefly until seeds are fragrant and onion begins to turn translucent. Stir often to avoid garlic burning.

Add the carrots, cabbage, chickpeas, vinegar, and water. Cover and let cook over medium heat for 30 minutes. Stir to prevent sticking. Add salt and pepper to taste.

Baked Lemon Ginger Tofu
Serves 6

2 - 8-oz packages firm tofu
2 lemons
2 tablespoons fresh ginger, grated
¼ cup tamari

2 tbsp. apple cider vinegar
¼ cup olive oil
Pinch of salt, pepper, and thyme

Pre-heat oven to 425°.

Drain the tofu and pat dry with a paper towel. Cut tofu into 1-inch cubes and place them into an ungreased a 9"x 13" baking dish.

Grate the outside of the lemons to create a large amount of zest (up to you how much – taste preference.) Add it to a bowl along with the juice from the lemons, ginger, tamari, vinegar, olive oil, and spices. Whisk together well and pour over the tofu. Shake back and forth to coat.

Cover with tinfoil and bake covered for 30 minutes, then uncovered for 15 minutes.

Fried Tofu with Dill
Serves 6

2 - 8-oz packages firm tofu
½ cup balsamic vinegar
1 cup. olive oil
1 tsp mustard powder

½ tsp turmeric powder
½ bunch fresh dill, chopped
Salt
Pepper

Drain the tofu and pat dry with a paper towel. Cut tofu into 1-inch cubes and place them into a metal bowl. Add the vinegar, oil, mustard powder, turmeric, salt, and pepper. Let sit for at least 20 minutes, and up to an hour.

Heat a bit of oil in a frying pan and then add the tofu, frying for five minutes, and stirring occasionally to prevent burning. Once finished cooking, add chopped dill and toss together.

ROASTED SQUASH AND GREEN LENTIL SALAD
Serves 6 – 8

2 cups dried green lentils
1 kabocha squash
3 tbsp. olive oil
2 cloves garlic, minced
1 tbsp. dried rosemary
2 tsp dried oregano
1 tsp paprika
¼ head of cabbage, sliced thin and then chopped into small squares

2 stalks celery, halved and sliced
2 tbsp. fresh ginger, grated
2 tbsp. honey
1 tsp dried mustard
Salt and pepper to taste
1 bunch fresh cilantro, chopped

Pre-heat oven to 400°.

Cut squash in half and scoop out seeds. Peel the skins as best you can (they are quite tough!) and cut into bite-size cubes. In a large bowl, toss squash with the olive oil, garlic, rosemary, oregano, and paprika. Place onto a greased cookie sheet and bake for 30 minutes.

Cook lentils by placing them in a saucepan and cover with 2" of water. Bring to a boil, then reduce to a simmer and cover, stirring occasionally, for 20 minutes, or until lentils are just cooked. They should retain their shape. Drain and set aside.

Dissolve the honey and mustard together by adding a touch of boiling water. Mix well. Then stir in the ginger.

In a large bowl, combine the cabbage and celery. Add the cooked lentils, roasted squash, and honey mixture. Add cilantro, salt, and pepper and toss together.

Tempeh and Kale
Serves 3 - 4

1 lemon
1 orange
1 tbsp. fresh grated ginger
2/3 cup tamari
1/3 cup oil

Salt and pepper to taste
1 - 12-oz package tempeh, thinly cubed
1 bunch kale, roughly chopped
1 package of frozen peas

Pre-heat oven to 375°.

Grate the skins of one lemon and one orange, then juice the fruit. Whisk together the zest, lemon and orange juices, ginger, tamari, oil, salt and pepper.

Place the tempeh and kale into a baking dish. Add the marinade and shake to coat all pieces. Then cover tightly with tinfoil and bake for 30-40 minutes. Remove from the oven and stir in the peas, cover again for at least 10 minutes for the peas to cook through. You shouldn't need to return it to the oven in order for the peas to cook, but you can do so to keep it warm until you serve.

Basic Frittata
Makes 1 8" cast-iron skillet

8 eggs
3 tbsp. milk
1 tbsp. olive oil
2 tsp dried dill

1 ½ cups chopped vegetables
¼ cup shredded cheese
Salt and pepper
1 tbsp. butter

Pre-heat oven to 375°. Put the 1 tbsp. of butter into the cast iron skillet and put inside oven as it warms.

Sauté the vegetables in a little bit of oil to cook them. If you are using a tomato or avocado, you don't need to cook it first. However, if using something like broccoli or mushrooms, cooking first is the way to go! This is also an ideal way to used left-over cooked vegetables.

Beat the eggs, milk, oil, spices, salt, and pepper together until well mixed.

Take the skillet out of the oven once it's hot. Spread the vegetables (either cooked or uncooked) evenly over the bottom of the skillet and pour the egg mixture over the top. Because the skillet is already hot it will set the bottom and sides of the egg mixture. Sprinkle the cheese over the top.

Place skillet back into oven and bake uncovered for 15 minutes, or until middle is set. You can also cover the skillet with a pot lid before placing it in the oven – this will ensure a faster cooking time. However, the lid should not cover the pan tightly, which will result in the egg mixture rising up uncontrollably like a souf-flé! Have the lid slightly askew.

Avocado, Tomato, and Goat Cheese Frittata

Makes one 8" cast-iron skillet

8 eggs
3 tbsp. milk
1 tsp curry powder
1 tsp oregano
½ tsp salt

½ tsp pepper
1 tomato, chopped
1 avocado, cubed
4 ounces goat cheese
1 tbsp. butter

Pre-heat oven to 375°. Put the 1 tbsp. of butter into the cast iron skillet and put inside oven as it warms up.

Beat the eggs, milk, curry, oregano, salt, and pepper together until well mixed.

Take the skillet out of the oven and scatter the tomatoes and avocado evenly on the bottom. Pour the egg mixture over the top and swirl it around. Scatter small pieces of goat cheese on top.

Place skillet back into oven and bake uncovered for 15 minutes, or until the middle has set.

Falafel
Makes 20 falafels

2 cups dried chickpeas, soaked overnight	*1 cup brown rice flour*
1 yellow onion, quartered	*2 tbsp. olive oil*
4 cloves garlic	*1 tsp salt*
1 jalapeno pepper	*1 tbsp. cumin, ground*
1 bunch parsley or cilantro	

Pre-heat oven to 350°. Line 2 9x13" baking sheets with parchment paper, or lightly grease with olive oil. No need to grease if using parchment.

Drain the soaked chickpeas and set them aside.

Using a food processor, pulse together the onion, garlic, jalapeno, and fresh herbs until they are chopped; do not over blend or the mixture will turn to liquid. Pour this into a bowl.

Now add the chickpeas to the food processor and pulse together until the mixture becomes fine, but still retains the shape of small sand granules. Add this to the bowl with the onion mixture, along with the flour, olive oil, salt, and cumin. Mix well.

Form round patties by pressing the falafel batter between the palms of your hands, and using your thumb to shape the edges. They should be roughly 1" tall and 1.5" wide. Place them on baking sheets and bake for 40 minutes, turning the patties over halfway through cooking.

You can also refrigerate this batter for up to 2 days in the refrigerator before using.

Adzuki Beans
Serves 3 – 4

1 cup dried adzuki beans
1 onion, chopped
1 tbsp. fresh grated ginger
2 carrots, sliced diagonally

1 stalk celery, sliced diagonally
1 tbsp. cumin seeds
½ tsp salt
1 bunch fresh cilantro, chopped

Rinse adzuki beans. Add them to a pot and cover with 2" of water. Bring them to a boil, then cover with a tight fitting lid, and simmer for 60-90 minutes, or until beans are soft. More water may be added while beans are cooking if they appear dry. The beans will become thick and break apart a little bit as they finish cooking.

While beans are cooking, heat a bit of oil in a saucepan. Fry the onions briefly, then add the carrots, celery, ginger, and cumin seeds. Reduce heat and cook, stirring often, for 15 minutes.

Once beans are finished cooking, add the carrot mixture and salt to the cooked adzuki beans and stir together. Garnish with cilantro.

DILLED AND SPICED GARBANZO BEANS
Serves 3 – 4

1 ½ cups dried garbanzo beans
(or 2 14-oz cans)
1 onion, chopped
4 carrots, sliced diagonally and
very thinly
1 tbsp. coriander seeds

1 tsp turmeric powder
1 bunch fresh dill, chopped
1 tbsp. fresh grated ginger
3 tbsp. water
Salt to taste
Olive oil

Soak the garbanzo beans for at least 6 hours or overnight.

Drain the garbanzo beans and add them to a saucepan. Cover with 2" of water and bring to a boil. Scrape the foam off the top and discard. Reduce to a simmer and cover with a tight-fitting lid, cooking for 60-90 minutes, or until beans are soft. Strain and pour into a small baking dish.

Near the end of cooking the garbanzo beans (alternatively, if you are using canned beans, this can be done right away) pre-heat oven to 350°.

Heat a bit of olive oil in a frying pan. Add the onion and cook for a few minutes, until it begins to turn translucent. Add the carrot and coriander seeds as well, and cook together until coriander seeds begin to pop. Remove from heat and pour into the baking dish along with the garbanzo beans.

Add the turmeric, dill, ginger, water, and salt to the beans as well. Bake for 15 minutes.

RED LENTIL DAL
Serves 4

1 ½ cups dried red lentils	1 tsp coriander
1 tbsp. oil or ghee	1 tsp fenugreek powder
2 tomatoes, chopped	½ tsp turmeric powder
4 cloves garlic, sliced very thin	Pinch of cinnamon
2 tsp cumin seeds	Fresh cilantro for garnish

Rinse the lentils well, until the water runs clear. Cook the lentils by adding them to a pot with about 4 cups of water, the coriander, fenugreek, turmeric, and cinnamon. Bring to a boil, and then reduce to a simmer for about 15 minutes. Don't stir them as they cook. Lentils will break apart and become soupy. Once they finish cooking, take a whisk and place it into the lentils. Twirl the whisk back and forth between your palms. This will give the lentils a creamier texture.

In a separate pan, heat the oil or ghee. Add the cumin seeds and heat until they begin to pop. Then add the tomatoes and garlic, and heat for just another couple minutes, stirring often so that the garlic doesn't burn. Remove from heat. Add to the lentils and give a brief stir. Salt to desired taste. Garnish with chopped cilantro if desired.

Split Chaana Dal
Serves 4

1 tbsp. butter
1-2 onions, chopped
3 cloves garlic, minced
2" ginger, minced
2 tsp mustard seeds
½ kabocha squash, peeled, deseeded and cubed

6 cups water
½ tsp turmeric
1 tsp coriander powder
1 tsp fennel powder
1 cup split chaana (split garbanzo beans)
Salt and pepper to taste

Rinse the chaana with cool water until the water runs clear. Set aside.

Heat butter in a saucepan. Add the onions and sauté over medium heat for 7-10 minutes, stirring often to prevent burning. Add the garlic, ginger, and mustard seeds and heat for another 3 minutes or so, stirring, until mustard seeds begin to pop. Add the kabocha squash, water, and the rest of the spices (turmeric, coriander, and fennel). Bring to a boil, then reduce to a simmer, uncovered for 10 minutes. Add the split chaana and simmer again for 40-60 minutes, partly covered. Stir every now and then and add more water if needed. When finished cooking, add salt and pepper to taste.

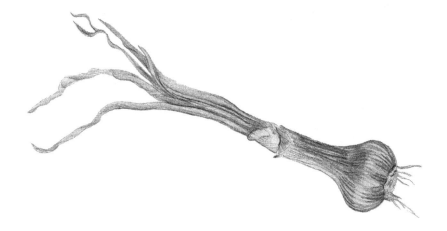

LENTIL PATTIES
Makes 6 patties

This recipe is a great way to use up leftover lentils and/or rice. It works best with lentils that are thicker in texture, so you may want to strain out excess liquid if possible. You can always make lentils and rice fresh for the purpose of this recipe, but we find it's a great way to try something new after a meal already was enjoyed!

2 cups leftover dal or lentils
1 cup cooked rice, white or brown
1 cup brown rice flour
1 onion, chopped very fine

1 tsp salt
1 tsp curry powder
2 tsp olive oil
1 bunch fresh cilantro, chopped

Pre-heat oven to 350°.

 Using a food processor, pulverize the rice. Add the lentils, flour, onions, salt, curry, oil, and cilantro. Pulse together until the mixture looks uniform. If the mixture is soupy, add more flour or rice.

Form patties with the palms of your hands and place onto a greased baking sheet. Bake for 30 – 40 minutes, flipping the patties halfway through cooking.

Mung Bean Curry with Toasted Coconut
Serves 4

½ cup flaked coconut
1 ½ cup dried mung beans
1 tbsp. coconut oil
1 onion, chopped
2 cloves garlic, minced
1 jalapeno pepper, minced

8-oz coconut milk
½ tsp white pepper
½ tsp turmeric power
1 tsp cumin powder
1 tsp coriander powder
¼ tsp clove powder

Toast coconut in the oven: Pre-heat oven to 300°. Place coconut onto a cookie sheet and cook for 15 minutes, or until coconut becomes slightly browned. Careful not to overcook!

Cook mung beans by placing them in a pot with about 5 cups of water and a bay leaf. Bring to a boil, then reduce to a simmer and cook for 40-50 minutes.

In a small bowl, mix together all the spices: the white pepper, turmeric, cumin, coriander, and clove.

In a separate pan, heat the oil. Add the onion, garlic, and jalapeno. Stir often and cook until onions turn translucent. Add the spice mixture along with the coconut milk. A paste-like consistency should form. Heat for a minute or so, then stir into the cooked mung beans, along with desired salt.

Sprinkle with toasted coconut on top.

The Kindness of Chickens to the Human Race
By Andy Wistreich

When I was young, I learned to love the taste of chicken. I guess that many of us did. My Jewish grandmother would cook me chicken soup with noodles, and it was a kind of comfort food. When my mother was getting old and I would visit her from time to time on my own, she would cook roast chicken as a treat for me, knowing I was vegetarian and didn't get it at home, and I couldn't say no because I needed to accept her kindness. She wanted to please me. It was an act of love on her part.

Even when I was young, but much more so today, almost every chicken eaten on the planet is raised in an industrial poultry farm. The birds are genetically modified to produce more breast meat, as a result, they are top-heavy, can barely stand, and often break their legs. They are kept in close confinement, either on a barn floor or in a cage, shut away from natural light, and subjected to accelerated day and night using lamps. Their life is very unnatural. They are fed continually with anti-biotics to reduce the danger of disease and their beaks are trimmed to stop them from pecking out the eyes of their neighbors. Imagine how frustrated, angry and tortured they must feel, and how this leads to aggressive behavior towards their neighbors. Many die early, and when those that live come to the slaughter-house they are killed most brutally.

Research by the University of Bristol in England shows chickens to be intelligent creatures, with emotions, and who make choices. Those who raise chickens in their backyard, in the old-fashioned way, know this. They can develop a personal relationship such that the chicken gladly runs to the human when they meet. When I met some well-cared-for chickens at a friend's place, they came up to me; I am sure with smiles in their eyes.

Fifty billion chickens are consumed every year by the seven billion people of this earth. They suffer immeasurably to service our appetites. They are appreciated by humans in general, not as living beings, with personality and feelings, but simply for their taste. Imagine if another species treated us like that!

Many of us have experienced the pleasure of enjoying the meat of chickens. We ought to feel grateful for what they have done for us, spending their lives in pain and torment, and eventually dying, simply to become our food. Our pleasure arises on the back of their suffering.

Farming poultry wasn't always an industry. The first such poultry farm was created in 1932. The idea quickly caught on because it enabled mass production of chicken at a low price. We might be tempted to blame the farmers for their greed, but actually the public who crave cheap meat are equally responsible.

Personally, I am vegetarian these days, so I could adopt a self-righteous attitude that the poultry industry isn't my responsibility. However, as a human being, I am one of the species that is oppressing the chickens. Moreover, my healthy body of today owes something to the protein derived from chickens when I was younger. On reflection I find that I cannot escape my role in this process.

I don't like to get emotional about this issue, as it clouds one's judgement, but I can't help feeling that of all the atrocities on the planet (and we know there are many), the poultry industry must be high up the scale. It is unbelievably cruel. It is hidden from view, in buildings in the countryside all over the planet, to which very few outsiders ever gain access. We get so upset about concentration camps and other forms of cruelty by humans to humans, but rarely consider the way we are abusing so many chickens, our fellow sentient beings. The vibrations from this activity are everywhere, and they are not pleasant. They are part of the overall energetic fallout of aggression that is discernible at a subtle level everywhere.

There used to be a poultry farm owned by Tibetans near Bylakuppe in South India. His Holiness the Dalai Lama was giving teachings there, and reported that he had been kept awake at night by the screams of the chickens which he found distressing. As a result the Tibetans decided to close down the factory, and they therefore needed to dispose of all the chickens. They decided to sell them very cheap – twenty rupees each – on condition that they would not be killed. People bought them for their eggs. In that area there are many mongooses, and these, like foxes, are famous for killing and eating chickens. However, not one of the released chickens was ever killed by a mongoose. The Tibetans said that this was because they were under the protection of His Holiness!

What I have written applies similarly to pigs, cows, salmon, and other species factory farmed for food. I hope we will all become more conscious of these beings as worthy of our love and compassion. They are treated as components in an industrialized process, and completely stripped of their identity as feeling, sentient beings. Children grow up, not associating what is on their plates, with those delightful creatures they see in films or in the farmyard. It is as though we are living in a collective dream, hidden from the reality of what our species is doing to those we exploit.

I often meditate on the chickens, and am moved to tears. Please remember them in your meditations and prayers. Maybe one day we can develop a kinder world.

Andy is an English Buddhist practitioner, who is vegetarian, and aspiring to become vegan since learning more about industrial farming. He has led retreats at Vajrapani Institute whose founder, Lama Yeshe, was one of his teachers. It was Vajrapani Institute's director, Fabienne Pradelle who woke Andy up to the reality of factory farming through giving him the book ‹Eating Animals› by Jonathan Safran Foer.

Soups

Soups are one of my favorite foods to cook. There is no way to isolate a vegetable or herb in a soup; the essence of each ingredient will pierce the entirety of the broth, with or without puréeing. There are no walls and no boundaries between the ingredients. Creating a soup involves bringing tastes together in a flavorful and harmonious blend, and it's never quite the same each time. Soups have a way of completely embracing one ingredient with another, and this can lead to a pensive look upon one's face as they questioningly decipher each hidden flavor.

Soups are also a great way to use up the mis-matched vegetables you have in your kitchen. Go ahead, open your fridge, peer inside, and see what you can collect: one large carrot, three zucchini, and a handful of parsley. Now look atop your counter, what else can you add? Two sweet potatoes, one yellow onion, and a thumb of fresh ginger. Once your vegetables are prepared, sauté the ingredients in a little bit of butter beforehand to draw out their flavors, then add a liquid like vegetable stock, canned tomatoes, or coconut milk, and simmer together for at least 40 minutes.

As a beautiful look unto relational existence, when making a soup we can ask ourselves, how does a collection of tastes compliment itself? How does sweet potato soup become even more than just sweet potatoes? When I add ginger into the sweet potato soup, the two tastes become inextricably linked in a dependent fashion that renders a soup "whole," yet it's a new whole, beyond mere sweet potatoes and beyond mere ginger.

You may say that all recipes involve this blending of flavors amongst the ingredients. You may point out that this theme of "bringing tastes together" happens in every meal, regardless of how ingredients are combined. And you would be right, to an extent – yet what fascinates me most about soups is that they involve a complete dissolution of one ingredient into the other. Unlike a stir fry, where each ingredient is still an autonomous piece that can be pierced individually with a fork, in a blended soup there are none of these extracted pieces which have not invariably contaminated the entirety of the dish with its own essence. In this way, these blends of vegetables stand out as a special concoction in the kitchen – effectively merging two tastes, two essences, into a new combined whole.

How to Make Your Own Vegetable Stock

Making your own vegetable stock is a way to customize the flavor of your soups or curries; and it is a wonderful alternative to using stock cubes, which often contain loads of salt or MSG.

There are a few ways to go about making vegetable stock, but in essence, it's super simple: put some vegetables in a pot, cover with water, bring to a boil, and simmer together for 30-40 minutes. Then strain out the vegetables. If you aren't planning on using it within 3 days, store in the freezer and thaw when you need it. Here are a few ways to do this:

∞ If you are doing a lot of cooking at one time (say, for a holiday or dinner party), you can have a "stock pot" nearby while you cook. Place scraps of onion, carrot, celery, fennel bulb, fresh herbs, and garlic into the pot. Throw in a couple bay leaves, then cover with water, bring to a boil, and cook for about 30-40 minutes. Strain out the veggies and pour the liquid into a sealed container.

∞ Save your vegetable scraps over a period of time and freeze them. After you cook and have your onion peels, carrot peels, and bits and pieces of celery, continue to add them to a gallon Ziploc bag that you keep in the freezer. Once the bag is full, add the contents to a pot and boil it in some water. Then strain out the vegetables.

∞ Create your own stock by using whole vegetables. Roughly chop a couple onions, a few stalks of celery, and a handful of carrots and add to a stock pot. Fresh herbs, garlic, and ginger also work well but will alter the taste of your finished product, so keep that in mind! Add the vegetables to a stock pot with some water, boil, and cook together for 30 or so minutes. Strain out the vegetables.

CREAMY SQUASH AND ZUCCHINI SOUP

Serves 4

1 kabocha squash, peeled and cut into cubes	*1 tsp cumin seeds*
5 zucchini, chopped	*1 tsp coriander powder*
3 tbsp. butter or coconut oil	*½ tsp turmeric powder*
1 onion, chopped	*Salt and pepper*
4 cloves garlic, sliced	*8 cups vegetable stock or water*
1 jalapeno, chopped	

Heat butter or oil in a 2-quart saucepan until it's melted. Add the onions and sauté over medium-high heat for 10 minutes, stirring often. Then add the garlic, jalapeno, and cumin seeds, sautéing over medium heat for 2 more minutes. Add the kabocha squash, coriander, turmeric, salt, and pepper, and vegetable stock. Bring to a boil, cover, and simmer for 20 minutes. At this point, add the zucchini, and continue to cook together for another 15 minutes. You can add more water if too thick.

Using an immersion blender, blend the soup well until it is pureed to smooth perfection. Alternatively, you can use a regular blender, but be very careful when blending hot liquids.

BUTTERNUT SQUASH SOUP WITH TOFU
Serves 4

1 butternut squash, peeled and cubed
1 tbsp. coconut oil
1 onion, chopped
1 tbsp. fresh ginger, grated
2 cloves garlic, minced
1 tsp turmeric
1 tbsp. coriander

6 cups water
2 cups coconut milk
1 package extra firm tofu, cubed
3 zucchini, sliced
(optional) fresh cilantro and sour cream for garnish

Heat oil in a 2-quart saucepan until melted. Add the onion and garlic and sauté, stirring often, until onion is translucent. Add butternut squash, ginger, water, turmeric, and coriander. Bring to a boil then reduce to a simmer for 15 minutes, or until squash is soft.

While the soup is cooking, cut the tofu into cubes and fry separately until all sides are brown. Alternatively, you can steam the tofu before adding to the soup.

Stir the coconut milk into the butternut squash soup. Using an immersion blender, blend the soup well. Or if using a regular blender, puree the soup in batches, being careful about the hot liquid (you can always let the soup cool a bit first).

Return to the stove and add the tofu and zucchini. Heat the soup for another 5 – 10 minutes until zucchini is soft through.

Garnish with sour cream and chopped cilantro.

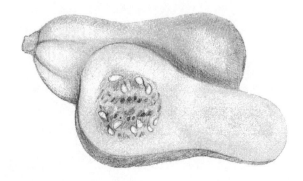

CARROT CASHEW SOUP
Serves 4 - 6

1 kabocha or acorn squash
2 tbsp. coconut oil
1 onion, chopped
2 tsp fresh ginger, chopped

2 cloves garlic, minced
2 lbs. carrots, peeled and sliced
½ cup cashews
4 – 6 cups stock or water

Soak the cashews by covering them with hot water for at least 30 minutes (longer is better). Once they are done soaking, strain them, and then add them to a blender along with 1 cup of fresh water and blend until smooth.

Pre-heat oven to 400°. Grease a cookie sheet with olive oil or put down parchment paper. Cut squash in half and scoop out the seeds. Place cut-side down onto the cookie sheet. Add a little water to the sheet pan as well, and then roast for 35-40 minutes, or until squash is cooked through. Let cool before handling.

In a 2-quart saucepan, heat coconut oil and add the onions, garlic, and ginger. Cook over low heat for a few minutes, until onions begin to turn translucent. Add the carrots and stock. Bring to a boil, and then reduce to simmer and cook for 20 minutes.

Once squash is cool enough to handle, scoop out the inside of the squash and add to the carrot soup. Also add the blended cashews. At this point, use an immersion blender until soup is smooth.

ROASTED RED BELL PEPPER AND TOMATO SOUP
Serves 4 – 6

1 onion, chopped
4 cloves garlic, minced
2 lbs. (3-4 large) red bell peppers
2 sweet potatoes, peeled and cubed
2 tsp dried oregano
1 tsp chili powder

1 tsp powdered fennel
1 28-ounce can of diced tomatoes
1 8-ounce can of tomato paste
4 cups stock/water
Salt to taste

Pre-heat oven to 400°. Cut bell peppers in half and scoop out seeds. Place them in a baking dish with high sides and drizzle some olive oil and a splash of water over the top of them. Cover the dish tightly with tinfoil and place in the oven for 40 minutes to an hour. Remove from the oven and let them steam for 10 more minutes before opening the foil and letting them cool. The skins should be very easy to remove. Do your best to remove all the skins once they are cool enough to handle; but it is okay if some of the skins do not peel off.

While the peppers are cooking, heat a bit of oil in a 2-quart saucepan. Add the onions and garlic and sauté together for a few minutes, stirring often. Add the potatoes, oregano, chili, fennel, tomatoes, tomato paste, and stock. Bring to a boil, and then simmer together for 20-30 minutes.

Add the bell peppers once they are roasted and peeled. Using an immersion blender, blend the soup well. Salt to taste.

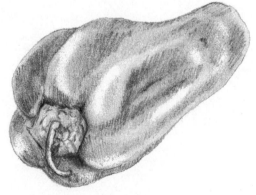

WHITE BEAN AND KALE STEW
Serves 4

1 16 oz. can white navy beans
2 tbsp. olive oil or butter
1 onion, chopped
2 cloves garlic, minced
1 tbsp. fresh ginger, grated
4 celery stalks, sliced 1/2" thick
4 tomatoes, chopped
1 8-oz can tomato paste

6 cups water or stock
1 tsp coriander
¼ tsp white pepper
2 tsp dried rosemary
1 tsp mustard powder
1 bunch dino kale, chopped
Salt and pepper, to taste

In a small bowl, mix together the spices: coriander, pepper, rosemary, and mustard powder, and set aside.

In a 2-quart saucepan, heat the oil or butter and add the onion, heating for about 3 minutes or until onions begin to turn translucent. Then add the garlic, pepper, ginger, and celery. Give a stir and heat for a few minutes more. Add spices, tomatoes, paste, water/stock, and beans. Bring to a boil and then simmer together for 10 – 20 minutes. Add chopped kale, salt, and pepper and heat for at least another 10 minutes.

Simple Tomato Soup
Serves 4

2 tbsp. olive oil
1 onion, chopped
4 cloves garlic, sliced
4 stalks celery, sliced
2 carrots, chopped
2 tsp dried oregano
1 tsp dried thyme

1 tsp chili powder
1 8-oz can of tomato paste
5 lbs. (5 large) tomatoes, chopped
6 cups water or vegetable stock
Salt and pepper to taste
1 large bunch fresh parsley or cilantro, chopped

Heat oil in a 2-quart saucepan over low heat. Add the onions and garlic first, heating for a minute or two, and then add the celery and carrots. Heat together, stirring every now and then, for 10 minutes. Add the chopped tomatoes, the spices, tomato paste, and stock or water. Bring to a boil, and then simmer together for 20-30 minutes more. You can either keep chunky as is, or blend well using an immersion blender. Add salt and pepper to taste.

Zucchini Garlic Soup
Serves 4 – 6

4 tbsp. butter
2 onions, chopped
4 cloves of garlic, minced
1 russet potato, cubed

2 ½ lbs. (about 7) zucchinis, chopped
8 cups vegetable stock or water
Salt and pepper
1 bunch parsley, chopped

Heat butter in a 2-quart saucepan until it begins to melt, and then add the onions and garlic. Keep over low heat for 10 minutes, until onions begin to brown. Stir often to prevent sticking, and keep over low flame to prevent from burning. Add the potatoes, zucchini, salt, and pepper, and add enough stock or water to just cover the vegetables. Bring to a boil, and then reduce to a simmer for 15-20 minutes, or until potatoes break apart. Add the chopped parsley and blend with an immersion blender until smooth.

Curried Sweet Potato Soup
Serves 4

2 lbs. (4-5 large) sweet potatoes, peeled and cubed
1 tbsp. butter
1 onion, chopped
4 cloves garlic, minced

1 14-oz can coconut milk
4 cups water or vegetable stock
1 tbsp. fresh ginger, grated
1 tbsp. curry powder
Salt and pepper

Melt butter in a 2-quart saucepan. Add the onion and cook for 10 minutes. Then add the garlic and ginger, stirring and cook for a few minutes more. Add the potatoes, coconut milk, water, and curry powder. Bring to a boil, and then reduce to a simmer, covered, for 20 minutes. Using an immersion blender, blend the soup until it reaches a creamy consistency. For a chunkier soup, you can also mash with a potato masher or stir with a whisk. The potatoes should be soft enough that they fall apart easily. Add salt and pepper to taste.

POTATO SPINACH SOUP
Serves 2 - 3

1 tbsp. butter
1 onions, chopped
2 stalks celery, sliced
3 cloves garlic, minced
1 lb russet potatoes, peeled and cubed

3 ½ cups water or vegetable stock
2 tsp marjoram
1 tsp salt
¼ lb fresh spinach

Melt butter in a saucepan. Add the onions, celery, and garlic; cook them over low heat for 10 minutes. Then add the potatoes, water or stock, and marjoram. Bring to a boil, then reduce to a simmer, uncovered, and cook for 15 minutes, or until potatoes are soft all the way through. Turn off heat. Add the salt and spinach, and stir until spinach wilts. Using an immersion blender, blend the soup well until perfectly smooth.

FOOD OFFERING PRAYER

The following three prayers are in accordance with the three paths of practice in the Tibetan Buddhist tradition. The first prayer represents the individual path, the second, the universal path, and the third, the mystical path. Prayers one and three were compiled by Venerable René Feusi. The second came about from our annual Family Camp.

To Buddha, the teacher of happiness

To dharma, the path to happiness

To sangha, the helpers on the way to happiness

I offer this delicious food

By this may all beings find happiness

And enjoy the food of calm-abiding

As craving leads to unhappiness

I will eat without craving

Mindfully and peacefully

∞

Thank you all living beings

For giving us this food

May it nourish us

So that we may nourish others.

∞

This food and drink

Purified, actualized and increased

By the three vajra-syllables

Become an ocean of bliss-void nectar

Om Ah Hum (3x)

In the lotus at my heart

Gurus and buddhas

To you I offer

This bliss nectar

Please bless me

To achieve vajradhara-union

In this life

∞

Venerable René Feusi was ordained in 1985; in 1988 he began a 5-year period of study at Nalanda Monastery followed by a 2 1/2 year retreat. Following the experiential lineage of Lama Yeshe and Lama Zopa Rinpoche, Venerable René now teaches worldwide and helps his students get an intuition of their own inner potential and inspires them to become meditators themselves. Venerable René lived at Vajrapani Institute for 7 years as our precious Resident Teacher.

Salads & Salad Dressings

I remember the first time someone asked me to make a salad dressing; I was completely at a loss, having no idea where to even begin. Salad dressings were something that came in bottles from grocery store shelves, and had a long list of ingredients and emulsifiers and preservatives. How was I to make my own?

Once I learned that salad dressings stem from the simple combination of oil and vinegar, much of my salad dressing stress was alleviated. The mystery was no longer very mysterious, and I began to wonder why people always defaulted to buying salad dressings when they could get creative with their own.

The ratio of oil to vinegar is generally 4:1, and you can experiment using different types of oils, though olive oil is usually the go-to because of its delicious flavor that it brings to dressings, rather than something like canola oil, which is bland-tasting. There are also many types of vinegars to try, such as apple cider, balsamic, red wine, or brown rice.

With oil and vinegar as a base, you can add a thickener like mustard, tahini, or nutritional yeast; herbs like thyme or freshly cracked black pepper; sweeteners like honey or agave; seeds like poppy or sesame; citrus like lemon or orange; and even purée some fruit into the mix, like strawberries or figs.

Likewise with salads, after knowing your "base" of ingredients you can truly go anywhere with flavors. I enjoy making rich, creamy potato or egg salads as a side to a lunch meal. To begin, I chop up red onion, celery, a fresh herb like dill or parsley, and a handful of garlic, usually sautéed lightly in a generous amount of oil. Then add the mashed up egg, or cooked potatoes. Dollop your desired amount of mayonnaise and mustard on top with some salt and pepper and stir to combine. Alternatively to boiled eggs or russet potatoes, you can also use leftover plain pasta, sweet potatoes, or even winter squash. (When using potatoes or squash, I will roast them before tossing with the salad instead of boiling on the stovetop – I find they retain their shape much better, and the sugars from the vegetables are extracted from the roasting process which adds a nice flavor to the finished product.)

For green salads, once you have a base of mixed greens, lettuce, or spinach, you can pile atop raw vegetables, like shredded beets and carrots; cucumbers and tomatoes; even fresh or dried fruit like apples, pears, raisins, or figs.

COLESLAW
Serves 3 – 4

2 carrots, shredded
2 stalks celery, sliced thin
1 red onion, chopped
4 garlic cloves, minced
½ head of green cabbage, shredded
½ cup mayonnaise

2 tbsp. vinegar, apple cider or white
2 lemons or limes, juiced
½ bunch fresh parsley, chopped
Salt and pepper to taste
1 cup peas (optional)

Add all ingredients to a bowl, including the mayonnaise, vinegar, parsley, salt, and pepper. If you are using frozen peas, cook them according to package instructions before adding. Toss together. Refrigerate before serving.

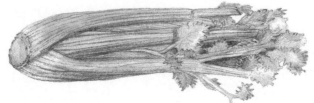

EGG SALAD
Serves 6

8 hard-boiled eggs
4 stalks celery, sliced very, very thin
1 red onion, chopped
1 bunch fresh dill, chopped
4 cloves garlic, minced

2 tbsp. Dijon mustard
½ - ¾ cup mayonnaise
1 lemon, juiced
Salt and pepper to taste

Peel the hardboiled eggs and add to a bowl. Using the back of a fork or a potato masher, mash them into chunks.

Add the chopped vegetables to the bowl with the eggs. Add the mayonnaise, lemon juice, and a bit of salt and pepper. Stir the mixture well and mash more if necessary. Taste for salt and pepper.

Raw Kale Salad
Serves 3 – 4

1 large bunch of kale
1 lemon, juiced OR 1 ½ tbsp apple cider vinegar
¼ cup + 1 tbsp. olive oil
2 tsp agave (optional)
½ tsp salt
2 carrots, shredded

1 red beet, shredded
½ red onion, sliced into thin half-moons
½ cup raisins
¼ cup sunflower seeds, toasted and crushed
½ cup shredded parmesan cheese (optional)

Rip the kale off of the stalk into bite-size pieces and into large bowl. Juice the lemon on top of the kale, and add the olive oil, agave (if using), and salt too. Using your hands, begin to massage the kale (yes, massage – squeeze kale tightly between your fists) until the leaves become softer, and an even darker green. The acid from the lemon juice or vinegar will help to break down the stiffness of the leaves.

Add the shredded carrots, onion, beets, raisins, seeds. Toss together and sprinkle the cheese on top (if using.)

Italian Salad
Serves 4 – 6

4 large tomatoes (beefsteak or heirloom), chopped
1 cucumber, peeled and cut into cubes
1 red onion, chopped very small
1 can of black olives, halved
2 cloves garlic, minced

1 lemon, juiced
¼ cup olive oil
1 tbsp. white vinegar
2 tsp dried oregano
Salt and pepper

Add the tomatoes, cucumber, onion, and olives to a bowl.

Whisk together the garlic, lemon juice, vinegar, olive oil, oregano, salt, and pepper. Pour over tomato mixture and toss together.

Mushrooms and Tomatoes
Serves 6 - 8

1 lb. white mushrooms, quartered
4 large tomatoes (beefsteak or heirloom),
chopped
½ onion, sliced very thin

2 cloves garlic, minced
¼ cup olive oil
2 tbsp. apple cider vinegar
Salt and pepper

Heat a little oil in a 2-quart saucepan. Add the mushrooms and sauté over medium-high heat for 5 minutes or so, stirring often, until browned.

Add mushrooms to a bowl along with the fresh tomatoes, onion, and garlic. Mix together. Drizzle olive oil and vinegar over the top, add salt and pepper to taste.

Spinach Salad
Serves 2

1 lb. fresh spinach
4 strawberries, sliced
2 carrots, shredded
½ red onion, sliced very thin
2 lemons, juiced
1 tbsp. olive oil

1 tsp mustard
1 tsp white vinegar
Pinch of salt and pepper
½ cup almonds, toasted and chopped
Feta cheese (optional)

Whisk together the lemon juice, olive oil, mustard, vinegar, salt and pepper. Set aside.

Place the spinach in a bowl and top with the strawberries, onions, carrots, and toasted almonds. Pour the dressing over the top and toss together. Crumble feta on top if desired.

COOL CUCUMBER YOGURT SALAD
Serves 4

1 cucumber, peeled and chopped
½ red onion, chopped
2 garlic cloves, minced
2 celery stalks, sliced thin
2 cups plain yogurt
3 tbsp. olive oil

2 lemons, juiced
1 tsp grated fresh ginger
1 bunch of fresh dill, chopped (or 2 tbsp. dried)
Salt and pepper

Add the cucumber, onion, garlic, celery, and dill to a bowl.

Whisk together the yogurt, olive oil, lemon juice, ginger, salt and pepper. Add to the cucumber mixture and stir together well. Add more lemon juice if desired.

ORANGE AND BEET SALAD
Serves 3 – 4

1 cup shredded beets	*2 tbsp. honey*
1 cup shredded carrots	*2 tbsp. hot water*
1 orange, juiced	*½ tsp powdered ginger*
1 lemon, juiced	*Salt and pepper*

Whisk together the honey and hot water. Add the orange juice, lemon juice, ginger, and a little salt and pepper.

Add the shredded carrots and beets to a bowl. Toss with the orange juice mixture briefly; if you mix for too long the beets will stain all the carrots purple! If this happens, it is okay – it will still taste delicious.

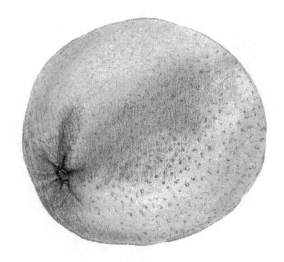

POTATO SALAD
Serves 6

4 russet potatoes

2 carrots, shredded

2 stalks celery, sliced very thin

2 cloves garlic, minced

½ cup mayonnaise

1 tbsp. Dijon mustard

1 tbsp. olive oil

½ tsp salt

1 bunch fresh dill, chopped

4 tbsp. chopped scallions

Wash potatoes well and keep skins on. There are two methods to cook them:

1. Pre-heat oven to 375°. Slice potatoes in half and slather with olive oil. You can either dip each potato half into a bowl of oil or brush the oil on. Then place potatoes face-down on an ungreased cookie sheet. Add ¼ cup water to the pan and place in oven for 30 minutes, or until potatoes are soft when poked with a fork. Remove from oven and let cool.

2. Alternatively, you can also cook the potatoes by boiling them. Cut them into 2 inch rounds. Add them to a pot and cover potatoes with cold water. Bring to a boil, and then simmer for 7-10 minutes, check to see if they are done cooking by poking them with a fork. Drain, and run cold water over them to cool.

Once potatoes are cool, cut them into cubes. Add the potatoes to a bowl along with the carrots, celery, garlic, and dill. Mix together.

Whisk together the mayonnaise, mustard, oil, and salt. Add this to the potatoes and mix together well. Garnish with scallions. Keep in the fridge until you are ready to serve.

Spinach Salad with Egg Dressing
Serves 3 - 4

For the salad:
1 lb. fresh spinach, chopped
3 hard-boiled eggs (white part only)
½ cup almonds, toasted and chopped

For the dressing:
3 hard-boiled eggs (yolks only)
½ cup sour cream
1 tbsp. Dijon mustard
¼ cup of water
1 lemon, juiced
1 tbsp. rice vinegar
Salt and black pepper

Separate the egg yolks from the egg whites. Chop the white parts and add to a bowl with the chopped spinach. Use the egg yolks for the dressing.

To make dressing, mash the egg yolks with the sour cream and mustard. Add the water, lemon juice, and vinegar and whisk together with a fork until smooth. Add salt and pepper to taste.

Add the dressing to the spinach and stir to coat. Then garnish with the toasted almonds.

Pico de Gallo

4 beefsteak tomatoes, chopped into small pieces
1 yellow onion, chopped
3 cloves of garlic, minced
1 jalapeno, minced

1 tsp dried oregano
1 bunch fresh cilantro, chopped
1 lemon, juiced
3 tbsp. olive oil
Pinch of salt and pepper

Add the tomatoes, onion, garlic, jalapeno, oregano, and cilantro to a bowl. Over the tomato mixture, pour the olive oil and lemon juice, and then sprinkle with salt and pepper. Mix together.

SALAD DRESSINGS

Use a blender to combine the following ingredients together. Alternatively, you can use a whisk and mix by hand, or add to a ball jar and shake well.

HOLLYHOCK DRESSING

¼ cup water

¼ cup soy sauce

1/3 cup apple cider vinegar (or balsamic)

2 cloves of garlic (optional)

1 cup nutritional yeast

1 cup olive oil

CREAMY BALSAMIC VINAIGRETTE

½ cup balsamic vinegar

½ cup water

1 tsp mustard powder

¼ cup tahini

3 tbsp. honey

salt and pepper

1 ½ cup olive oil

POPPY SEED HONEY-MUSTARD

¼ cup apple cider vinegar

1 lemon, juiced

3 tbsp. Dijon mustard

3 tbsp. honey

½ tsp thyme

½ tsp salt

¾ cup olive oil

2 tbsp. poppy seeds

LEMON TAHINI DRESSING

½ cup tahini

½ cup hot water

1 lemon, juiced

¼ cup rice oil

1 tsp agave syrup or honey

1 tbsp. apple cider vinegar

2 tbsp. Bragg's Liquid Aminos or soy sauce

A Practice for the Supermarket
by The Karmapa, Ogyen Trinley Dorje

You can consciously work on becoming a more enlightened participant in these food systems. One simple practice you could adopt is to briefly pause at the entrance to the supermarket, or wherever you shop for food.

Just take a moment to adjust your attitude. Instead of the usual approach – that you have come there to make purchases – tell yourself that you have come to make choices. Make the aspiration that your choices will make a difference for others. As you enter the store, envision that you are treading the same path as many other people who are similarly seeking to make wise choices. Then, as you walk through the store, keep in mind that the choices you are making form a crucial component of the food systems that deliver food to everyone in your society. What you see available on the shelves reflects what people have been choosing to buy. Every purchase you make will support certain food industries, and send a small signal of approval and acceptance.

While you are shopping, you can think of the kind of food options you would like everyone to have available to them, and put those items in your cart. You can even think of the kinds of food industries or practices you want to see changed, and keep their items out of your cart. As you do this, you can hold in your heart a hope that the choice you make today will join with the choices of other like-minded shoppers to bring lasting changes that will benefit many others, too.

If you approach food shopping in this spirit, you will naturally want to take some initiatives to better inform your choices. There is already a great deal of information available about commercial food products. It would be great if someone would create a phone app that would help us access and analyze all the relevant information about each item on supermarket shelves. Along with the list of ingredients, we need information about where each item comes from, how far it traveled, its impact on our health, how it was grown or slaughtered or manufactured, and how the company treats its workers. When you are standing in the supermarket, you could use this information to identify products that cause less suffering to your body, to animals, to humans, and to the environment.

It is up to us to educate ourselves not just on general issues of nutrition, but about the particular food items we are eating. This would allow us to better understand and anticipate the immediate and long-term consequences of our food practices. Actively seeking out and using sources of information about food products gives us alternatives and options. It can also send a clear message to big companies that we are aware of what they are doing, and ready to act on our awareness.

The fact that today there are vegetarian restaurants in many cities, and vegetarian options in many nonvegetarian restaurants, is visible proof that the food choices we make as individuals have the collective power to bring about change. After enough individuals inquired about vegetarian options, restaurant managers recognized that it was in their interest to add vegetarian selections to their menus. The same happened with organic foods in supermarkets. We should not underestimate our power to bring about change.

∞

The Karmapa is one of the highest-ranking lamas in Tibetan Buddhism and is the leader of Tibetan Buddhism's oldest reincarnation lineage. The present incarnation, Ogyen Trinley Dorje, is the seventeenth in this line. Since his escape from Chinese-occupied Tibet at the age of fourteen, he has emerged as an international Buddhist leader and environmental activist. He lives in Dharamsala, India, just a short distance from his mentor, His Holiness the Dalai Lama.

Credit: From The Heart is Noble: Changing the World from the Inside Out by Ogyen Trinley Dorje Karmapa, ©2013 by Ogyen Trinley Dorje. Reprinted by arrrangement with The Permissions Company, Inc., on behalf of Shambhala Publications, Inc., www.shambhala.com

Dips, Spreads and Sauces

Much like salad dressings, we often think of sauces and dips as foods which come straight from the grocery store, and I know from my own experience growing up, making my own sauce always seemed to be beyond my culinary reach. However, they usually are not very complicated to make, despite what the lengthy list of ingredients on the back of the can or jar will tell you. While it is certainly convenient to buy jars of tomato sauce as a way to throw together a quick meal, when making your own you have the freedom and power to design the flavor as you like it.

As far as using up leftovers, dips are a great way to use leftover casseroles or beans. I once cooked a delicate squash casserole and proceeded to throw the leftovers in the food processor with a little bit of coconut milk and more cheese – it created a smooth and naturally sweet spread for dinner rolls. Alternatively, you can always fry up some onions, throw them in the food processor with beans, and create a simple bean dip in under 15 minutes for a gathering.

Basic Olive Hummus

2 cups cooked chickpeas (approx. 1 can)
1/2 cup tahini
2 lemons, juiced
1/4 cup water
1/4 cup olive oil

1/2 cup pitted olives (black, kalamata, or green)
4 cloves garlic
1 tsp salt
1 tsp red chili flakes

For those of you who are not olive-fans, you can easily omit the olives and still have a tasty product.

First add the chickpeas into a food processor and blend for about a minute or so. Add the remaining ingredients and blend well for at least 2 minutes until perfectly smooth.

Delicata Squash Spread

2 delicata squash
2 tbsp. butter or oil
1 onion, chopped
2 tbsp. fresh ginger, grated
1 tbsp. curry powder

1/4 cup water
1/4 cup milk
1/2 cup shredded parmesan cheese
1/2 cup shredded swiss cheese
Salt and pepper to taste

Cut the squash in half and scoop out the seeds, no need to peel. Slice very thin.

Heat the oil or butter in a 2-quart saucepan. Add the onion and cook over medium heat for 10 minutes. Add the ginger, curry powder, squash, and water. Lower the heat and cover; cook for 20 minutes, or until squash is totally cooked through. Add the milk and cheeses and warm together for another 5 minutes. Add this mixture to a food processor and blend well.

AVOCADO SPREAD

2 cloves garlic, minced   *3 tbsp. nutritional yeast*
2 tbsp. olive oil   *1 tbsp. tahini*
2 ripe large avocados   *1/3 cup water*
2 lemons, juiced   *½ tsp salt*

Heat olive oil in a pan and add the garlic. Stir and cook over medium heat for less than a minute, just enough to get the garlic fragrant. Mash all ingredients together.

Goes great on toast! Or serve with sliced baguette bread at dinner.

Marinara Sauce
Makes about 2 quarts

4 lbs tomatoes, chopped
2 tbsp. olive oil
1 large onion, chopped
2 tsp fennel seeds
1 large (about 1/3 lb) carrot, chopped
2 stalks celery, chopped

2 tsp oregano
2 tsp salt
1 8-oz can of tomato paste
2 tbsp. olive oil
1 lb whole white mushrooms, sliced

In a heavy-bottomed pot, heat the olive oil, then add onions and fennel seeds. Cook over low-medium heat for 5 minutes. Add the garlic, carrots, and celery, and cook for 10 minutes more, stirring to prevent sticking. Add the spices, tomatoes, and tomato paste, and stir well until paste dissolves. The juice from the tomatoes should provide enough water for this to turn into a sauce. Keep the mixture over low-medium heat for another 20 minutes or so, until it's ready to blend. Using an immersion blender, puree the sauce until smooth. Cook together for 20 more minutes. Sauce should thicken a bit.

In a separate skillet, heat a bit more of olive oil or butter, then add the mushrooms and cook over medium heat for 15 minutes until they are very soft and juicy. Add them to the sauce either before or after you blend, depending upon if you want the chunks of mushrooms whole or puréed. This sauce will keep in the fridge for up to 5 days.

Broccoli Walnut Pesto
Creates 4 cups

1 cup walnuts
1 lb. broccoli florets
1 bunch fresh herbs, like cilantro, parsley,
or basil

4 cloves garlic
1 tsp salt
1 cup olive oil
1/2 cup grated parmesan

Toast walnuts in the oven: 15 minutes at 350° degrees.

Blanch* broccoli florets by boiling water in a 2-quart saucepan and then adding the broccoli to the water, but only for a minute or so. Broccoli will become bright green but still be hard to the touch. Drain. Alternatively, you can steam the broccoli for 2-3 minutes.

*Quick note on blanching: Broccoli's bright green color can fade if one cooks it for too long. If you put the broccoli in a pot of water first and then heat it up, the broccoli will turn a bleak and drab green. Thus, always boil the water before adding the broccoli. This will cook it for a brief period of time at a high temperature, retaining the beautiful color.

If using a food processor, place the toasted nuts, garlic, and herbs into a food processor. Blend well. Add the broccoli and salt, and pulse until the broccoli is nice and fine. Now with the food processor going, add the olive oil in a stream. Finally add the parmesan cheese and pulse a couple times to incorporate.

Without a food processor, chop the nuts, broccoli, herbs, and garlic by hand very, very fine; as finely minced as you can. Add them together in a bowl, along with salt and parmesan cheese, then top with olive oil and let it seep through.

You can easily turn this recipe into a pesto sauce for pasta as well. Just add it to a pot with 1-2 cups of milk and heat together. You may need to add a touch more salt. Cook pasta according to package instructions, and then toss it with pesto sauce before serving.

Zucchini Baba Ganoush
Serves 6

4 large zucchini, halved lengthwise
5 tbsp. olive oil
2 tsp salt
3 cloves garlic

5 tbsp. lemon juice
1 bunch fresh parsley or cilantro
1 cup tahini
½ cup water

Preheat oven to 450°. Toss zucchini with 2 tablespoons olive oil and a sprinkle of salt. Roast zucchini cut-side up on a baking sheet until golden brown and tender, 15 minutes. Remove and let cool.

Roughly chop zucchini. Add ¾ of zucchini and remaining ingredients to a blender or food processor and puree until smooth. To serve, top baba ganoush with remaining zucchini. Drizzle with olive oil and sprinkle with sea salt.

Any Bean Dip

1 14-oz can pinto, kidney, or black beans
1 large yellow onion, chopped
1 jalapeno, chopped
5 cloves garlic, minced

1 bunch fresh cilantro, chopped
2 tomatoes, diced
Salt and pepper

Heat a little oil or butter in a 2-quart saucepan, add the onions, jalapeno, and garlic and cook over low heat for 15 minutes, stirring often.

Put the beans, cooked onions/jalapeno/garlic, and cilantro into a food processor or blender. Blend well. Taste for salt and pepper. Transfer to a bowl and stir in diced tomatoes. Serve with chips.

Kitchen of a Yogini

by Elaine Jackson

In April 2014, I completed a three-year retreat. Prior to engaging in that retreat, I completed a month long solitary retreat every year for eleven years. Consequently, I've had a great deal of experience cooking for myself in retreat. I have always had the good fortune to have others volunteer to do the grocery shopping. Also during the long retreat, I had a garden that produced lots of produce and I canned plenty.

Simplicity is the key to eating a healthy diet while not spending countless hours in the kitchen. Buying bulk rice, beans and other grains you like is worthwhile. Once a week, I often cooked a large pot of soup with whatever vegetables I was harvesting at the time. Alternatively, I might make a casserole that was then eaten as the main meal all week. Since there were greens in the garden, a simple salad was an easy side dish. When I cooked rice, I made a large pot of it. I then heated it and re-heated it with soy sauce to use as a bed for lightly steamed vegetables. Having many canned tomatoes, pasta with a tomato-based sauce was quick and yummy.

Making corn tortillas was a cinch. Using Masa flour, salt and water, I'd mix a small batch, roll it into balls, flatten them with an inexpensive tortilla press, and fry them in a dry, non-stick skillet. This was great with beans, rice, salsa and a dollop of yogurt, which could morph into an enchilada casserole and serve as meals all week. Tortillas also served as a breakfast, warmed and slathered with peanut butter.

Breakfast granola was a favorite. I made fat-free granola by omitting butter and using water instead. In a saucepan I mixed one cup of brown sugar, one teaspoon of salt, one cup of water, and one tablespoon of cinnamon. After heating this until the sugar dissolved, I added one teaspoon of coconut extract (you could use vanilla extract, too) then I poured it over 6 cups of oats to which I had added, ½ cup sunflower seeds, ½ cup sesame seeds, ½ cup pumpkin seeds, ½ cup ground flax seed and 1 cup chopped nuts (walnuts, pecans, cashews, almonds – whatever I had). This is mixed well and baked on two cookie sheets (with sides) for about 30 minutes at 350°, turning every 10 minutes or so. When it is golden, remove it from the oven and add whatever dried fruit you have on hand. Let it cool completely, then store in a large jar with a lid. Eaten with a banana or other fruit, this makes a hearty, filling, delicious meal – morning, noon or night.

Evening meals were usually light and might be just fruit and yogurt or bread and cheese or a cup of hot chocolate. A savory plate of cheese, olives and celery stuffed with peanut butter was also an easy "grab it." Hard boiled eggs could be added, too.

Having just a few easy recipes that you like and can heat and re-heat, helps to keep cooking in retreat simple. Changing it up by adding nuts or fresh fruit or by drizzling a sauce over food keeps it from becoming a bore. The best piece of advice is to take the time to present it beautifully to yourself and then enjoy as much as possible. Know that you are feeding an Angel.

∞

Raising her family in a tepee on the land, Elaine Jackson is one of the early founders of Vajrapani Institute. She served as Vajrapani's executive director for five and a half years before retiring in 2009. Every year for 12 years she engaged in a month-long solitary retreat to deepen her practice. This was just prior to entering into a three year retreat which she completed together with her partner, Keith Emmons, in April 2014. Elaine now lives a contemplative life offering teachings and meditation support.

Desserts

Sweet tastes provide a simple, yet deeply profound, sense of satisfaction. While too much sugar can cause our blood sugar to go haywire, which not only can harm our meditation practice but our body in general, a treat with a sweet quality can be very comforting. Like most things in life, there is a balance to be struck.

In the recipes that follow, you will find that the amount of processed sugar is either very low or non-existent. Processed sugar is not needed for sweetness, and its concentrated quality makes it easy to go overboard when using. Keeping processed sugar to a minimum or replacing it completely with natural sugars (like stewed fruit) can be surprisingly tasty while not putting a strain on our bodies: excess of sugar has been shown to have taxing effects on our liver and kidneys, just like alcohol, as well as impeding our immune response.

Sweets are not inherently bad for us. We love the taste of ripe fruit for a reason; the sweetness means something good for our bodies. However, the overabundance of candy bars and cookies can become a problem if we over-indulge.

Homemade treats are a great way to cut down on sugar consumption, yet keep the sweet flavor alive in our hearts (and our bellies). Baking an item yourself gives you the choice and power to alter the amount of sugar you want to use.

In short, there are a few non-processed sugar aids that can help add a sweet flavor to your finished product:

Vanilla extract, pure cocoa, dates, ripe bananas, dried fruit in general, and applesauce, to name a few.

If you are an avid baker, try cutting down the amount of sugar that goes into your cookies and cakes. You may find that the texture changes a little bit; but the flavorful blast of the sugar is still present, even if it whispers instead of shouts.

The following recipes are also marked with a "V" or "GF," which denote a vegan or gluten-free recipe, respectively. I find that desserts are one area which can often be inaccessible to people who avoid dairy and gluten. To overcome the challenge of baking separately for those with special dietary needs, we have developed dessert recipes which can satisfy most, if not all, of the patrons who come through Vajrapani Institute. For this reason, most of our baked goods will be either vegan and/or gluten-free in nature. Even if you are not someone who avoids dairy or gluten, these recipes still prove delicious; the following recipes are for everyone.

In the following recipes you will also find frequent use of flax seed meal as an egg substitute. Not only can flax seed be sprinkled on top of your morning cereal for an added source of omega-3, but when whisked together with a small amount of water or milk, the flax meal becomes a binding substance in baked goods. In general, 2-3 tbsp. of flax seed meal can replace 1 egg. If you do not have flax seed meal on hand, you can always use the more common ingredient of eggs instead: roughly 2 eggs per ¼ cup flax seed meal listed in the recipes.

APPLE CINNAMON LOAF (V)
Makes 1 loaf pan

¼ cup flaxseed meal
1 cup soymilk
½ cup rice bran oil
1 tsp vanilla extract
½ cup brown sugar
2 – 3 apples, cored but unpeeled
1 lemon
1 cup all-purpose flour*

½ cup whole wheat flour*
1 tsp baking soda
½ tsp salt
2 tsp cinnamon
¼ tsp cardamom
¼ cup each raisins and walnuts
Poppy seeds (optional)

Pre-heat oven to 350°. Lightly grease 1 loaf pan. Sprinkle poppy seeds (if using) around the bottom and edges of the pan.

Shred the apples and squeeze the juice of one lemon on top. Set aside.

In a small bowl, mix together the flour, baking soda, salt, and spices.

In a separate bowl, put the flaxseed meal, milk, oil, vanilla, and sugar. Whisk mixture together very well until all the oil is incorporated. Add the flour mixture and blend until just combined. Stir in the shredded apples, raisins, and walnuts. Pour into the prepared pan and bake for 55-60 minutes.

This loaf comes out more like a cake than a bread. Cut the finished product into 6 squares and serve with vanilla ice cream.

*You can substitute 1 ¼ cup brown rice flour + 1/3 cup tapioca starch to make this recipe Gluten-Free.

Banana Bread (V)
Makes 1 loaf pan

¼ cup flaxseed meal
1 ½ cups soymilk or coffee
3-4 ripe bananas
1 tsp vanilla extract
¼ cup organic sugar
½ cup rice bran oil
2 cups all-purpose flour*
1 tsp baking soda

2 tsp cinnamon
1 tsp allspice
½ tsp salt
½ cup chocolate chips or raisins (optional)
1 tbsp. molasses
Coconut oil (for greasing the pan)
Sesame seeds (optional)

Pre-heat oven to 350°. Generously grease 1 loaf pan with coconut oil. Sprinkle sesame seeds on the bottom of the pan.

In a small bowl, mix together flour, baking soda, spices, and salt.

In a separate bowl, mash the bananas well. Add the soymilk or coffee, flaxseed meal, vanilla, sugar, and oil. Beat well, or use a whisk to mash and combine the mixture until it is uniform and all the oil is incorporated. Add the flour mixture and beat another couple minutes until combined. Stir in chocolate chips if using. Pour into the prepared pan and drizzle the molasses on top of the batter in a zig-zag fashion. Bake for 55-60 minutes.

* You can substitute 1½ cups brown rice flour + ½ cup tapioca starch to make this recipe Gluten-Free.

Banana Oat Cookies (V)
Makes 16

4 ripe bananas
¼ cup molasses
3 cup rolled or quick oats*

1 tbsp. cinnamon
½ tsp nutmeg
¼ tsp baking soda

Pre-heat oven to 350°. Grease a baking sheet, or line it with parchment.

If using rolled oats, pulse the oats in a food processor until they are coarsely chopped. Add the spices, baking soda, and salt, and pulse to mix. (If using quick oats mix these ingredients together in a bowl.)

In a separate bowl, mash the bananas with the back of a fork. Add the oat mixture and stir until combined. Drizzle the molasses mixture into the batter and give a quick stir – don't completely incorporate the molasses to give it a swirl-look.

Using a spoon, drop dollops of the batter onto the baking sheet. Press down with the back of a spoon or fork to make them flattened a bit. Bake for 8 – 10 minutes, or until bottoms are golden brown. Cookies will be soft and chewy.

* This recipe can be made Gluten-Free if you use certified Gluten-Free oats.

Did you know…

Oats themselves do not contain gluten; however, they are often processed on equipment that also processes flours containing gluten. For this reason, if you are extremely sensitive to gluten, you must buy certified gluten-free oats, which are processed on uncontaminated machines.

CHOCOLATE CHIP BANANA COOKIES (V)

Makes 24 cookies

½ cup cocoa powder

¼ cup coconut oil

4 ripe bananas

1 cup crunchy peanut butter

1 tsp cinnamon

2 tsp vanilla extract

2 ½ cups quick-cooking oats

Pre-heat oven to 375°. Place parchment paper on a couple of baking sheets, or lightly grease them with coconut oil.

In a bowl, mash the bananas very well. Add the cocoa, coconut oil (it should be solid – if you live in a warm place where is has melted, put it in the fridge to firm it up), peanut butter, cinnamon, vanilla, and oats. Mix together well. The batter will be thick and sticky. This is good!

Drop into large dollops onto the baking sheet. Flatten a little with the back of a spoon. Bake for 15 minutes.

Peanut Butter Oat Cookies (V)
Makes 24

¾ cup chunky peanut butter
3 ripe bananas
1/3 cup rice bran oil
1/3 cup flaxseed meal
1/3 cup honey
2 tsp vanilla extract
2 ¼ cups rolled oats

¾ cup brown rice flour
¼ cup tapioca starch
1.5 tsp baking powder
1/2 tsp salt
2 tsp cinnamon
1/2 tsp nutmeg

Pre-heat oven to 350°. Place parchment on two baking sheets.

Whisk together dry ingredients.

In a separate bowl, blend together the rest of the ingredients. Add the dry ingredients to the wet, stir together, and then add in raisins and mix again. Drop in large spoonfuls onto baking sheet and bake for 12-14 minutes.

CRISPY ZUCCHINI MUFFINS (GF, V)
Makes 12

2/3 cup applesauce
1/3 cup ground flaxseed meal
¾ cup milk
2/3 cup rice bran oil
1 1/3 cup shredded zucchini
2 cups gluten-free flour*

3 tbsp. organic sugar
1 ½ tsp baking powder
½ tsp salt
1 tbsp. dried thyme
1 tsp cinnamon

Pre-heat oven to 400°. Oil muffin tins.

Mix together dry ingredients: the flour, sugar, baking powder, salt, and spices.

In a separate bowl, whisk together the applesauce, flaxseed, milk, and oil for two minutes, until the batter is uniform and oil is incorporated. Add in zucchini and mix well.

Pour dry ingredients into wet ingredients and mix until combined. The batter will be very thick; do not over mix. If you need to, add 1 tablespoon of milk more. Scoop into prepared muffin tins; the batter will be full in each tin. Bake for 30-40 minutes, until the tops look mountainous and browned. Let them cool completely; they will become crispy on the outside, but soft on the inside!

* You can substitute 1½ cups brown rice flour + ½ cup tapioca starch to make this recipe Gluten-Free.

Zucchini Carrot Muffins (V)
Makes 12

2 cups all-purpose flour*
1 tsp baking powder
1/2 tsp baking soda
1/2 tsp salt
1 tsp cinnamon
1/2 tsp nutmeg
1/2 tsp cardamom

1 cup shredded carrots
½ cup shredded zucchini
1/3 cup coconut oil, melted
2/3 cup soymilk
1/3 cup organic sugar
1 cup unsweetened applesauce
1 ½ tsp vanilla

Pre-heat oven to 400°. Oil the muffin tins or line them with muffin sheets.

Whisk together the dry ingredients: the flour, baking powder, baking soda, salt, and spices, and set aside.

In a separate larger bowl, mix together the oil, milk, sugar, applesauce, and vanilla. Stir well until oil is incorporated. Briefly stir in the shredded carrots and zucchini. Add in the dry mixture and mix just until combined - do not over mix or muffins can become gummy. It's okay if it's a little lumpy.

Pour the mixture into prepared muffin cups, approximately 2/3 of the way full. Bake for 20-25 minutes.

* You can substitute 1½ cups brown rice flour + ½ cup tapioca starch to make this recipe Gluten-Free.

Pear Crisp (GF, V)
Makes 11x13" pan

8 ripe pears	*¼ cup brown sugar*
2 lemons	*1 tbsp. cinnamon*
½ tsp cardamom	*½ tsp nutmeg*
Pinch of salt	*Pinch of salt*
2 cups oats	*½ cup coconut oil*
2 cups brown rice flour	*½ cup soymilk*

Pre-heat oven to 350°. Generously oil the baking dish with coconut oil.

Cut the pears into thin slices. Zest whole lemons, then juice, adding both the zest and the juice to the pears. Toss with cardamom and salt as well. Add these to the baking dish.

In a separate bowl, mix together the dry ingredients: the oats, flour, sugar, cinnamon, and nutmeg. Add the coconut oil (solid) on top. Using your fingers, break apart the coconut oil and mix into the dry ingredients. You will get a crumb-like consistency; this is good. Sprinkle mixture on top of pears. Drizzle the milk over the top of the entire dish. Bake for 45 minutes.

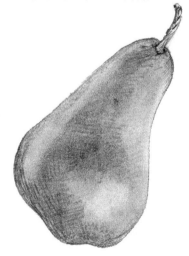

Squash Chocolate Pudding (GF, V)
Serves 4

1 kabocha squash	*4 ounces bittersweet chocolate*
8-oz coconut milk	*2 tsp vanilla*
1/3 cup cocoa powder	

Pre-heat oven to 400°. Oil a baking sheet or line one with parchment paper. Cut squash in half and scoop out the seeds. Place cut-side down onto baking sheet and roast for 30 minutes, or until squash is soft when pressed. Let cool. Once you are able to safely handle the squash, scoop out the insides into a large bowl.

Using a double-boiler, melt the bittersweet chocolate. Remove from heat. Add this to the squash along with the cocoa powder, vanilla, and coconut milk. Beat the mixture together until well combined. Serve with whipped cream or top with berries.

Nectarine Cobbler (GF, V)
Makes 11x13" baking dish

6 nectarines, chopped	*1 ½ cup gluten-free flour*
1 cup water	*1 cup chopped dates*
¼ cup brown sugar	*¾ cup soymilk*
1 tbsp. potato starch	*½ coconut oil, melted*

Pre-heat oven to 350°. In a saucepan, add the nectarines, water, sugar, and starch. Heat together over medium flame for 10 minutes, the mixture will thicken as it bubbles. Pour this into the ungreased baking dish.

Stir together the flour, dates, soymilk, and oil. Mixture will be lumpy because of the dates, but should be relatively uniform. Pour over the nectarines and spread evenly. Bake for 30 minutes, or until top is browned.

Carrot Loaf (V)
Makes 1 loaf pan, or 6 muffins

1 cup all-purpose flour*	*¼ tsp salt*
1 tsp baking powder	*½ cup coconut oil, melted*
1 tsp baking soda	*1 cup brown sugar*
2 tsp cinnamon	*½ cup flaxseed meal*
½ tsp allspice	*2 cup shredded carrots*
¼ tsp of clove	*2 tsp vanilla*
¼ tsp nutmeg	*¼ cup raisins*

Pre-heat oven to 350°. Grease one loaf pan and sprinkle sesame seeds around the edges. You can also make 6 individual muffins out of this mix.

Whisk together the dry ingredients: the flour, baking powder, baking soda, spices, and salt.

In a separate larger bowl, whisk together the oil, sugar, flaxseed meal, and vanilla. Do this until mixture is uniform. Stir in carrots. Add the dry mixture to the wet mixture and stir well. Stir in raisins and pour into prepared pan. Bake for 20 minutes if using a loaf pan. If you are making muffins, bake for 25 – 30 minutes.

* You can substitute ¾ cups brown rice flour + ¼ cup tapioca starch to make this recipe Gluten-Free.

STRAWBERRIES AND BANANAS IN CREAM (GF)
Serves 4

1 lb. strawberries
2 firm bananas
½ cup of sour cream

3 tbsp. milk
3 tbsp. sugar, honey, or agave
Juice of 1 lemon

In a bowl, mash the bananas with the sour cream. Add the milk, sweetener, and lemon juice. Stir together. Chop the strawberries and stir them into the mixture. This is best when served chilled; put in the fridge for at least 30 minutes before serving.

SPICED APPLESAUCE (GF, V)
Serves 2

1 lb. apples, cored but unpeeled
1 very ripe pear, cored but unpeeled
½ lemon
½ cup water

½ tsp cinnamon
¼ tsp allspice
Pinch of salt

Chop the apples and pear; add them to a saucepan. Juice the lemon over top, and then add the water, spices, and salt. Bring to a boil and then reduce to simmer for 15-20 minutes, or until apples/pear are soft and can be mashed. Use either an immersion blender or a potato masher to blend apples/pear. Serve warm, or pour over any dessert.

Scones (V)
Makes 12 scones

3 cups all-purpose flour*
2 tsp baking powder
¾ tsp baking soda
1 tsp salt
3 tbsp. sugar
6 tbsp. coconut oil

½ cup chopped pear/apple
1 lemon or orange, zested
½ cup soymilk + 1 tsp apple cider
vinegar (this will create 'buttermilk')
½ cup water

Preheat oven to 400°. Oil a baking sheet or line it with parchment paper.

Mix dry ingredients together: flour, baking powder, baking soda, salt, and sugar. As best you can, cut the coconut oil into smaller pieces and work them into the dry ingredients with your fingers. (If you are in a warm climate and your coconut oil has melted, put it in the fridge to solidify it before using.) Try to mix with your fingers as briefly as possible so the heat from your hands doesn't cause the oil to melt. The mixture should resemble coarse crumbs.

Add the chopped pear or apple and zest. Give a stir. Then pour the soured milk and water over the mixture and stir very briefly until it's barely combined.

Drop from spoon sticky globs of dough onto baking sheet. Bake until nicely browned, 15-20 minutes.

* You can substitute 2 1/3 cups brown rice flour + 2/3 cup tapioca starch to make this recipe Gluten-Free.

Gluten-Free and Vegan Baking

Why Gluten-Free?

Many of you may be conscious of the term "gluten-free," or "wheat-free." Gluten is a protein most commonly found in wheat, barley, and rye, and is responsible for the elastic and emulsifying property of bread. Ingesting it can cause internal inflammation in those with celiac disease, which is a severe form of gluten intolerance. Nowadays many people present symptoms of gluten sensitivity, including but not limited to: bloating, gas, fatigue, headaches, joint pain, sleeping difficulties, foggy thinking, and even those which mimic Irritable Bowel Syndrome. There are arguments on whether these symptoms are caused by eating gluten itself, or just an over consumption of gluten – as humans we have been eating gluten-containing grains for thousands of years; why are we so challenged by it today?

Gluten is a hard-to-digest protein, meaning we need a strong digestive system to break it down properly. If our digestion is compromised in some way, the undigested gluten can irritate our intestinal walls. It's also argued that gluten is not meant to be eaten three times a day every day all year round. If we are ingesting gluten more than we can handle, we will tax our body's ability to digest it properly, therefore creating an imbalance in our whole system. Though gluten itself may not be the culprit, our eating practices surrounding it may be part of the problem. Some people find that a gluten-free lifestyle allows them to get back to a state of digestive health.

Gluten-Free Flour Mix

Now that people are baking for gluten-sensitivities, there are many gluten-free flour mixes available for substituting all-purpose flour in your favorite recipes. It's important to keep in mind that gluten-free baking will be different than baking with all-purpose flour, but your end result should not be tough, crumbly, dense, bitter, or generally unappetizing. This defeats the purpose of baking a tasty treat.

However, there is some bad news: gluten-free flour mixes can be costly. The good news is that it's entirely possible to mix your own, and it won't break your wallet. What you will find below is Vajrapani Institute's recipe for their gluten-free flour mixture.

When baking with gluten-free flours, keep in mind that many of them have an added taste that all-purpose flour doesn't have. The reason for the blandness of white flour is that it is not a whole grain. There are two parts of the grain, the bran and germ, which are removed before the flour is ground into powder. (Those parts have a lot of nutritional value, yet they are removed to preserve the whiteness and concentrate the gluten protein in the flour.) What is left is the endosperm, which is primarily starch and protein. The protein, or gluten, is what makes our baked goods fluffy, spongy, and able to rise properly.

So when creating a gluten-free flour mix (and the recipe that follows is just one of many ways of doing so), you become a mixologist. Since all-purpose flour is a combination of starch and protein, those are what you'll want your gluten-free mix to have as well. You will be mixing whole-grain flours (high in protein, but not gluten protein), such as rice flour, buckwheat flour, chickpea flour, amaranth flour, corn flour, or millet flour, with a starch, such as potato starch or tapioca starch.

These ratios were determined by comparing the weight of the gluten-free mix to that of all-purpose flour. Cooking by weight gives more of a guarantee that the result will come out the same each time.

> *1 cup of All-Purpose Flour = 5.2 ounces*
> *1 cup of Gluten-Free Flour should also equal 5.2 ounces*
>
> *Rice Flour to Starch Ratio = 3 : 1*

So for every 3 cups of rice flour, you will use 1 cup of starch. Easy, right? This mix can generally be used in baked goods and as a thickener in soups or curries, but not in breads or dough which require rising.

GLUTEN-FREE FLOUR MIX RECIPE

3 cups brown rice flour
3 cups white rice flour
1 cup tapioca starch
1 cup potato starch

Sift all ingredients together; make sure they are evenly mixed.

Cooking Vegan:
Egg, Milk, and Butter Substitution Suggestions

Egg Substitutes

Egg substitutes can be used in most baked goods. The function of the egg in most recipes is to bind or add moisture, and that is why it is an essential ingredient in so many desserts. Without eggs, many desserts would crumble, or lack the moisture to be bound together. Flaxseed meal is the most commonly used substitute in the VPI kitchen, which we have found is a fail-safe method for holing sweet breads and cookies together. In addition, there are many other options involving puréed fruit.

Keep in mind, however, that egg substitutes of puréed fruit will only work well if the recipe has minimal eggs and also contains baking soda and/or baking powder. A recipe which contains many eggs, such as lemon bars, have a harder time substituting this way.

To replace 1 egg:

With Flaxseed Meal:
Blend together
2 tbsp. flax seed meal
3 tbsp. water

With Banana:
1 banana, blended

With Applesauce:
1/3 cup applesauce

With Fruit:
3 tbsp. pureed fruit

Milk Substitutes

Coconut milk, rice milk, almond milk, and soy milk can all be used in place of cow's milk in many recipes. Keep in mind that the taste of the finished product will be affected. I find that in curries and soups, it is best to use coconut milk in order to preserve the rich and smooth taste that using whole milk would provide.

Butter Substitutes

In many baked goods, butter can be replaced with equal parts of either earth balance or oil, like coconut oil, rice bran oil, or canola oil. Generally for baked goods, coconut oil and earth balance work most effectively because they are solid at room temperature. However, we have had success using rice oil in cookies and sweet breads as well.

APPENDIX

KITCHEN TIPS

Re-appropriate food: Also known as, "using leftovers," re-appropriating food that you have previously made will help cut down on food waste and ease your time in the kitchen. For example, if you make a large pot of rice and lentil curry one evening, you can use the leftovers to create "lentil patties" which you can fry or bake the next day and top with sliced tomato and yogurt sauce.

Start where you are: An idiom made famous by many Buddhist practitioners, this saying also applies to the kitchen. If you are thinking of cooking up a meal but don't know where to begin, open your pantry and fridge and see what you already have on hand. This might give you ideas or insights into what is possible for you to make, while using up some of the resources you currently have available to you.

Stock up on staples: There are certain foods that you can guarantee you will eat with a fair amount of consistency. Grains such as rice, millet, pasta, kasha and oats; a variety of dried or canned beans; condiments like olive oil, coconut oil, balsamic vinegar, apple cider vinegar, tamari, and nutritional yeast; raisins, nuts, flours… Buy ball jars if you need to and store these items nicely in a cupboard or pantry. Having ingredients available and on hand enables you to use them more readily.

Shop light and often: Buying a small amount of groceries every other day allows you to know you will use them in your meals. It also will prevent over-crowding in your fridge, which often leads to forgotten produce that goes bad and is eventually thrown out. Having staples stocked up, as mentioned in the previous tip, also allows you to shop light and often.

Leave your kitchen clean: The process of cooking will inevitably messy your kitchen area, but cleaning up is important, because the next time you walk into that space, you want to inspire yourself with a clean and inviting workspace. There is nothing more deterring than a sink full of smelly dishes and a sticky countertop. Keep your cooking space a respected area.

Knife Sharpener: You can invest in a simple knife sharpener for $10 - $20 in any store that has a good kitchen supply section. Depending on how frequently you cook, you can sharpen your knives once a week to maintain ease with cutting, slicing, and chopping.

Chef's Knife: You may have seen professional cooks carry around a whole bag full of knives. Yes, in professional culinary environments, a wide range of knives can be used to prepare a meal. However, you may only need 3 variations of knives in your home kitchen, the most useful of which is the Chef's Knife. You can get a great knife for as little as $40, which, when properly cared for, is a great investment that will last you for years.

Food Processor: This item makes foods like hummus, falafel, bean dip, and mayonnaise easily and swiftly attainable for you to create in your kitchen. You can also shred and/or slice a large amount of raw vegetables very quickly.

Immersion Blender: Perfect for blended soups. You can blend the soup while it is hot and right in the pot – no transferring needed to a blender.

Blender: That being said, blenders are very useful for large batches of salad dressing and smoothies.

Citrus Press: Citrus is a great addition to roasted vegetables, a pot of black beans, or freshly made guacamole. A press makes it easy to squeeze half a lemon or lime on anything you have freshly prepared to give it an extra lift.

Garlic Press: Perfect for adding fresh garlic into salad dressings, pastas, or curries. The press maintains the pungent taste of garlic without dissipating all its juices over your cutting board.

ACKNOWLEDGMENTS AND REJOICING

This cookbook began as a small seed; an idea, a mere waft of inspiration. The coming of its existence is a dependent-arising of many motivational factors.

A huge thank you to the FPMT's spiritual leader and guide, Lama Zopa Rinpoche. His unending and ever-expansive kindness, as well as his intense desire to benefit others is utterly inspiring.

Big, big thanks to all the contributors who offered their beautiful writing in the articles of this book: Lama Zopa Rinpoche, Venerable Tenzin Chogkyi, the 17th Karmapa, Ogyen Trinley Dorje, Elaine Jackson, Andrea Lieberstein, Nina Tomkiewicz, and Andy Wistreich; also to those who contributed their own unique recipes: Kelli Peacock, Ruth Saro, and Nina Tomkiewicz; to the editor, Wanda Sinsroy; to Chris Wesselman, the talented photographer; to the graphic designer, Alexandra Stein, for her inspiring creativity; and to all the staff and community at Vajrapani Institute for their Big Love and constant support.

Thank you to Lama Yeshe and his abundance of heart. He continues to inspire our goodness even long after his death in 1984, for he gave his life to the well-being and spiritual growth of all beings, a gift of love which only multiplies as time goes on. The ripples of his positivity are beyond comprehension, and are no doubt found in every page of this cookbook.

Big Love

Bibliography

Center for Disease Control and Prevention. Carbohydrates. Retrieved from http://www.cdc.gov/nutrition/everyone/basics/carbs.html

Douillard M.D., J. Secrets to Enjoying Gluten Again. Retrieved from www.lifespa.com.

Fenster PhD., C. (2005).Cooking Free: 200 Flavorful Recipes for People with Food Allergies and Multiple Food Sensitivities. New York, New York: The Penguin Group.

Flynn, K. (2011). The Kitchen Counter Cooking School. New York, New York: The Penguin Group.

Hanley, L. (2011, May 11). List of Protein Rich Leafy Vegetables. Retrieved from www.livestrong.com.

Natural Epicurean Academy of Culinary Arts. 6 Tastes of Ayurvedic Food. Retrieved from www.naturalepicurean.com.

Paturel, A. (2014, December 7). The Truth about GMOs. Retrieved from www.webmd.com

Quinn, E. (Updated 2014, December 16). How Carbohydrates Provide Energy for Exercise. Retrieved from www.sportsmedicine.about.com.

USDA National Nutrient Database for Standard Reference, Release 27. Retrieved from http://www.healthaliciousness.com/articles/beans-legumes-highest-protein.php.

Weil M.D., A. The Dirty Dozen Plus. Retrieved from www.drweil.com

13556245R00088

Printed in Great Britain
by Amazon.co.uk, Ltd.,
Marston Gate.